GUNS
THE RIGHT WAY

**INTRODUCING KIDS
TO FIREARM SAFETY
AND SHOOTING**

JERRY LUCIANO

Published by

Gun Digest® Books, an imprint of F+W Media, Inc.
Krause Publications • 700 East State Street • Iola, WI 54990-0001
715-445-2214 • 888-457-2873
www.krausebooks.com

To order books or other products call toll-free 1-800-258-0929
or visit us online at www.gundigeststore.com

ISBN-13: 978-1-4402-4298-4
ISBN-10: 1-4402-4298-4

Designed by Sharon Bartsch
Edited by Corrina Peterson

Printed in United States of America

10 9 8 7 6 5 4 3 2 1

Related Titles

GUN SAFETY IN THE HOME
by Massad Ayoob

DEFEND YOURSELF:
A Comprehensive Security Plan
for the Armed Homeowner
by Rob Pincus

www.GunDigestStore.com

Foreword

Teaching the next generation to shoot is nowhere as easy as it used to be. Single-parent households, anti-gun sentiment, over-scheduled kids and lack of access to places to hunt and shoot all present obstacles. Yet, as Jerry "Ace" Luciano argues persuasively in Guns the Right Way, every child should learn gun safety, whether he or she becomes a shooter or not. Guns the Right Way tackles these problems and many more. How old should a child be before learning to shoot? Who should be his or her teacher? How do you teach important lessons about guns? You'll find thoughtful, thorough answers to these questions inside.

Ace Luciano estimates he has been involved in teaching over 10,000 kids to shoot- as a parent, as a Boy Scout leader, then as a board member of the United Sportsmen's Youth Foundation, and finally as director of the USYF and Wisconsin DNR-sponsored "Youthfest."

Before any of that happened, Ace was one of a bunch of University of Iowa students who I sometimes shot skeet with. He asked me for advice in getting started as an outdoor writer. "Keep writing," I told him, and he did.

The result is this book. I hope you enjoy it.

Phil Bourjaily
Author
Writer
Shotguns Columnist- Field and Stream Magazine

Contents

CHAPTER ONE

Children and Firearm Safety

©National Shooting Sports Foundation, Inc.

Growing up, I never believed it would happen to me, but it did. I have become my father. I find myself talking more and more about the good old days and yearning that the circumstances of my youth be available for my children. Due to advances in transportation and, most of all, technology, that will never happen.

When I was young, it was common to allow a youth to take and shoot BB guns, pellet rifles, .22s and even 20-gauges whenever they wanted. All summer long my friends and I roamed our rural neighborhoods with "dangerous" weapons like guns, knives and bows. Nobody ever got hurt, either intentionally or accidentally.

In high school, I regularly had my shotgun in the trunk of my car after hunting for an hour or so before school. That saved a trip home to retrieve it (and waste valuable hunting time) if I planned to hunt again after school. I also carried a Swiss Army knife in my pocket from the time I was seven years old, including to school (and that was often loaned to a teacher who needed to cut something). It never caused trouble, nor was I ever punished for "weapons violations" despite being quite a "little scrapper" growing up.

I was taught from an early age that things like guns and knives were tools that, when used properly, were an essential part of our everyday lives. Just like my baseball bat and the hammer in my Junior Tool Kit, they had a distinct purpose for which they were designed and were NEVER to be used inappropriately. I was taught that not only could that hurt somebody, but it would result in the removal of said tools, most likely for an extended period and with additional, punitive consequences!

I was also a member of the first generation to grow up in the computer age, but computers were certainly not an everyday part of life. The home computer was a simple keyboard with a floppy disk attachment called a Commodore 64, and it was used for only the most basic of games or for typing and doing papers and bookwork.

There was no such thing as the Internet when I was a child, nor would there be for over 20 years. The first home video game, the Atari 2600, was introduced and shortly thereafter it was accompanied by games that involved shooting. They were nothing like the shooting games of today, which are three-dimensional, in first person, and so realistic it's like you're standing behind the shooter looking over their shoulder, but shooting nonetheless. (More detail on the benefits and consequences of shooting games, as well as some interesting research, is discussed in Chapter 6.)

I mention this to demonstrate how popular shooting is in our culture. It is an enjoyable pastime and Olympic sport, an integral part of hunting and outdoor

Shooting can be a fun and safe form of recreation.

lifestyle, and it permeates our daily lives through the media − in the television, movies and video games that our children spend hours with every week.

This is why it is essential that every child learn at least the basics about firearms.

Our world is still a very dangerous place. In going about their everyday lives, children are exposed to dangers at every turn. Bicycles. Cars. Stoves. Kitchen knives and utensils. Stairs. Swimming pools. Trees. Baseball bats. Hockey sticks. Hairdryers. Curling irons. Doors. Windows, etc.

From a very early age we teach our children not to touch the hot stove. We teach them to look both ways before crossing the street. We teach them that the bat used in their little league game should never be used to swat their friend Johnny when he annoys them.

Why is it that we look at guns in society so differently?

I am of the firm belief that if every child were taught the rules of gun safety in the most basic form, it would have a severe and permanent impact on the incidence of injuries and even violent events that occur in this country every year.

I fondly remember the public-service announcements by Dick Van Dyke when I was a child that talked about the dangers of fire and repeated the mantra "stop, drop and roll." Why are there not commercials on television today that say when you see a gun to "Stop. Don't touch. Tell a grownup"? For all the so-called "concerns" of the folks out there who are anti-gun, you would think we would already have something along those lines, and shame on us for not doing it ourselves.

We teach our children not to touch things like stoves and irons. We teach them not to play with matches. If a child lets curiosity get the best of him or her and touches that hot surface, they are very quickly and permanently taught a very valuable lesson. Where is the case that a child touches something hot and dies from it? It really doesn't happen.

That is not the case with a firearm. One second of curiosity can lead to a lifetime of regret, and that is something no child should have to live with for his or her entire life.

Why should every child learn the basics of firearm safety? For many reasons, but these three in particular:

JUST AS KNOWLEDGE IS POWER, A LACK OF KNOWLEDGE CAN BE DANGEROUS, EVEN DEADLY

Can you imagine taking a child who has had formative experiences playing with harmless reptiles and insects such as garter snakes and crickets, and turning that child loose into a room with cobras and scorpions? (As we discuss later, toy guns can have a similar effect.) We teach our children about the dangers of fire, heat, automobiles, knives, bats, hammers, lakes and rivers, and even crossing the street! Why do we not want the same level of safety taught regarding an object that is found all over the country, numbering in the hundreds of millions?

CHILDREN, BY NATURE, ARE CURIOUS

We all know what curiosity did to the cat… But children's curiosity is a GOOD thing. It is the basis of how they learn, as well as the drive to continue learning. Ask 100 parents what the number one agitating question their child asks is, and it will be fairly unanimous… WHY? The English Philosopher, John Locke, is quoted as saying, "Curiosity in children is but an appetite for knowledge. The great reason why children abandon themselves wholly to silly pursuits and trifle away their time insipidly is because they find their curiosity balked, and their inquiries neglected." It is, therefore, our duty as adults, parents and members of society to allow and encourage curiosity in children in order to come to their own conclusions and gain and expand knowledge.

IT IS OUR DUTY TO TEACH THEM, WHETHER WE OWN GUNS OR NOT

As adults and stewards of a safe and common society, it is our duty to prevent the taking of unnecessary risks in the aforementioned quest for knowledge. It is the right thing to do to keep everybody safe. When taught the proper and safe use of firearms, children are exposed to another entire realm of knowledge, recreation, sport and skill. Perhaps most importantly, shooting is a fun and safe form of recreation and sport that can be enjoyed by all children for their entire lives.

It is my hope and wish that this book helps you to do that.

CHAPTER TWO

When Your Child is Old Enough To Handle a Gun

©National Shooting Sports Foundation, Inc.

Tell me if you've heard this advice: "Kids aren't responsible enough to shoot until they are 12 years old."

Or this one: "When I was a kid, I was given a single barrel 20-gauge and three shells and told to go out in the woods and bring back something for supper."

Or maybe even: "GUNS??? ARE YOU KIDDING??? Kids should NEVER be allowed to handle a gun and shouldn't even DRIVE until age 18!"

All of these opinions can, of course, be spot-on correct.

Each one can also be terribly wrong… because it depends on the child.

This, in my opinion (which has been honed over almost 40 years of shooting and hunting, and the instruction and introduction of thousands of youth over that period of time), is where there is a great disconnect that I believe can easily be remedied.

A study conducted on behalf of the Hunting Heritage Trust and the National Shooting Sports Foundation in January 2012 asked young people ages eight to 17 about how they viewed hunting and target shooting. A 385-page report on the survey showed results that were very clear. Young people who were exposed to hunting and shooting were more likely to have a positive view of those activities. Those who weren't exposed, well, weren't likely to have a positive view.

A warning to the reader – I am about to shock some of you.

As I write these words, I have four children ranging from 22 years to 10 years old. All of them shoot. All of them have their own firearms. All of them were not just introduced to guns and shooting, but active shooters by the age of…four.

I told you that you might be shocked. I ask that you bear with me so that I may explain.

You see, I have been an avid hunter and shooter my entire life, from age three. I started in my father's lap, aligning the sights on the chosen target and pulling the trigger while he held the Sheridan pellet rifle steady for me. Many times we punched holes in paper. Just as many times, we shot at empty "Jolly Good" pop cans that we saved from special events. Unlike today, pop was a rare treat in our house growing up. As I grew older, I would track down empty soda pop and beer cans from every possible place – friends, neighbors, even the side of the road. My mother relates the story of how once, as a six-year-old, I screamed at her to "STOP THE CAR!!!!!," then jumped out before it was even stopped and grabbed a paper bag on the side of the road that held a treasure of empty beer cans to shoot at as my target.

I was passionate. I was focused. Shooting was important to me and I did everything I could to participate in it whenever I could. I loved it because it was

Soda cans are inexpensive, readily available and fun to shoot.

something that my dad did, and something that has grown from that first day almost 40 years ago to something that we still do together today.

So, how does this relate to you knowing when your child is old enough to handle a gun?

The answer is, your child will tell you.

I showed curiosity, I asked questions, and when my father would shoot, I asked if I could try. All of those are signs of curiosity, of which children have no shortage.

Now, my father did not just hand me a gun and say "here you go kid," and walk away. Every interaction with a firearm was carefully controlled, with him not just present but in control of the gun for almost every second of the interaction. It was made to be fun and entertaining for short periods of time.

There was no stern lecture at the beginning telling me how guns were dangerous and how I was just a child and wasn't ready, nor were there any boring lectures throughout my budding shooting career beating the rules of safety into my head.

Remember, I was three years old. I just wanted to have fun with my dad.

Behavioral psychologist B.F. Skinner is known for his studies on conditioning and, more specifically, operant conditioning. Operant conditioning is different from classical conditioning in that it uses reinforcement and/or punishment to alter behavior. In his most famous experiment, Skinner conditioned a rat to push a lever by enticing it with food. Every time the rat pushed a lever, a food pellet was released. The rat ate the food. Before long, the rat was trained to get its own food.

Skinner also worked with and developed the process of negative conditioning in which an unpleasant thing was removed when a certain action was performed, such as tapping a button or pushing a lever.

Finally, there were studies involving punishment, in which there was a negative consequence after the act of performing a given activity.

I explain this theory not to wow you with my knowledge of behavioral science (it is actually rather limited), but rather to back my own theories with science. The lessons that were taught to me were subtle, yet effective. I was conditioned through positive reinforcement over time. One time we shot a full pop can with a pellet rifle. My father shook it up beforehand, unbeknownst to me, and when the pellet struck it exploded in a foamy spray that was amazing to a young child.

"Wow! That was really cool, Dad. Let's do that again!" We did, to the same effect.

My father took that opportunity to explain to me just how dangerous even this "little gun" could be to me, to my family, and to anybody that was at the wrong end of it. He stressed that never ever, ever, ever point this or any gun at anything that you do not want to kill or destroy forever.

As we shot, my dad would point out little things like, "This is the safety. We always keep this on until we are sure of our target and what's behind it so that we don't accidentally have the gun go off before we are ready to shoot."

My positive reinforcement was spending time with my dad and having fun.

Other things like the subject of hunting and killing animals also came up. There was a squirrel running across the yard and I wanted to shoot it. My father said "absolutely not." "Why?" I asked. "Because it is summertime and squirrel season is closed. We only shoot animals in the fall and only when they are in season. "Why?" I asked again. "Well, because those rules make sure that we aren't taking a mama squirrel away from her babies when she needs them when they are little in the spring. We also only take so many of them so that we do not shoot all of them and there are more squirrels for us to take and eat next year."

Again, little lessons over time.

Those lessons were burned into my brain over the course of years, repeated over and over again. Never a lecture, never a two-hour lesson, but, rather, periods of fun and enjoyment with a lesson going along.

As a child, it never occurred to me to ever do anything wrong or unsafe with a gun. Just as it never occurred to me to pick up a hammer and knock holes in

Many of us grew up with guns.

our walls. I was taught otherwise.

Fast-forward seven years: I had lots of friends, and the vast majority of them did not hunt or shoot. To me, this was a foreign concept. I lived in a rural area, with woods surrounding our home and a cornfield across the street. Having been raised with guns and hunting, it was perfectly normal for me to assume that that was what most kids did. It was also perfectly normal for me to assume that I could have my friends come over and shoot my pellet rifle or my shotgun with my father and me.

It turned out that this was not often the case.

My parents received some phone calls from parents of school friends who had come over and shot my pellet rifle in the backyard with me. Not all of them were good phone calls.

I had a friend named Dave who had never shot a gun before. Dave was from "the city" (Chicago) and spent summers out in our rural community with his grandparents. I will never forget the first thing he did when I handed him my pellet rifle to examine. He picked it up and turned it over, pointing the muzzle directly at me.

I hit the floor and screamed at him, "Point that gun up in the air!"

His response: "It's fine, it's not loaded."

We were eight years old.

Clearly, Dave was not yet ready to properly handle a firearm without some serious instruction. Just as clearly, I was at a different level of experience, knowledge and comfort.

Almost 20 years later, I had another experience that molded the way I, and someone who had been "anti-gun until they're adults," viewed kids and guns.

My son had a friend named Tim. Tim was a great kid and was a special child in many ways. One of those ways was that Tim was born with his left arm ending in two fingers instead of an entire hand. Tim also had a left leg that was shorter than his right, with only four toes on one foot, which was also a different size from the other. You would never know it by the way Tim acted, though. It didn't even slow him down.

They met in preschool and were basically inseparable for years until we moved away almost 400 miles to Michigan's Upper Peninsula. Once, Tim came up to stay with us for a bit and we went and did all kinds of fun things. We hiked in the woods, went out on the boat and went fishing. One of the things we wanted to do was go to a local abandoned gravel pit and shoot .22 rifles.

For that, and for all interactions with guns, I insist on having parental approval before doing anything. Tim's parents were divorced, and since Tim's mother had set up the visit and would be returning to her, we called Tim's mom and explained what we wanted to do. She had a complete meltdown and forbade him from going near any guns with me or anybody else. Tim was eight – the same age I had been in the experience with my friend Dave. I brushed it off and found other activities to distract the kids in order to avoid upsetting anybody.

I also have a steadfast rule – certainly for guns, but in everything that we do: I make the decisions for my children, you make the decision for yours. We may or may not agree, but your child is not my child and vice versa.

The week that Tim spent with us was wrapped up with a sleepover where a number of my son's friends came over to our house. Tim's mom came to pick him up and take him back home on a Sunday afternoon, but she wasn't going to go anywhere without giving me a lecture about kids and guns.

She began with the age-old, "Guns are dangerous, he could get hurt, I'm afraid of an accident," speech.

This is an important point to stop and reflect, as I find that the overwhelming driving force of parents who don't want their children learning about firearms is fear, and most often that fear springs from a lack of experience and knowledge. It is also a great opportunity to introduce two people to guns.

As the conversation moved forward, we got into the whole "he wants/ she wants" argument that evolved into what clearly were some parental and relationship issues that had nothing to do with guns. (Remember, Tim's parents were divorced, and if that is the case with any children you are teaching, make certain you have at least one parent's written permission. Trust me.)

I quietly interrupted her and said, "Let me show you something."

Five other local boys, friends of my son, were at the house. Those boys were up and down the stairs going between our playroom and my son's bedroom constantly, which required them walking through our living room. They all had been introduced to guns before, most of them having a great deal of shooting and/or hunting experience.

I took out my Ruger 10/22 rifle, triple and quadruple checked that it was unloaded, and carefully laid it on the coffee table in the middle of the living room with the action open. The rifle has a 3-9x magnification scope on it and a 25 round magazine that I intentionally left in to give it an even larger profile. Those boys went through that living room four or five times over the next hour while we had coffee in the kitchen. Every one of them ignored that gun lying in plain sight in the middle of the coffee table.

Every one, that is, except Tim. Tim stopped almost every time he went by and looked at the gun, even touching it a couple of times.

That is a dangerous situation, and that is why my kids are talked to about guns from a very early age in my home and why I advocate teaching kids as young as three about firearms. Unfortunately, we lost touch with Tim over the years, but I hope that he received some proper training, somewhere.

Your purchase of this book demonstrates that you have an active interest in teaching children about guns, and I believe my decades of experience when it comes to kids and guns will allow you to find it extremely helpful.

CHAPTER THREE

Introducing Young Children to Firearms

©National Shooting Sports Foundation, Inc.

The concept for this book came about because of the many questions I received from parents wishing to properly introduce their own children to firearms. The vast majority of those who had questions were parents of rather young children.

Some of the questions they posed included:
- What is the proper age for me to teach my child gun safety?
- When is it okay for a child to shoot a gun?
- If I have a gun in my house, am I asking for trouble?
- I'd really like to take up shooting, but my spouse says not until the kids grow older.

Growing up around firearms and hunting, much of what I learned about guns came from a mix of both active and passive learning. Certainly there were experiential learning opportunities as well as designated safety lessons, but there was also a great deal of reinforcement over a period of many years that is difficult to replicate in a how-to format. Do you set up your child to walk in when you are cleaning your firearm? What if you don't own your own firearm and simply want your child to have the experience and knowledge to remain safe and make their own choices about guns?

It posed a difficult dilemma.

The main issue I have found is that many people wishing to introduce their children to firearms have absolutely no idea how to begin. This book can be the foundation for your lesson plan to properly introduce your child to firearms.

Some might assume that keeping their children away from firearms is a way to keep them safe. Some might end up doing just that, never knowing that it was entirely the wrong path to take.

A key understanding here is to realize that keeping children from firearms and keeping children safe while properly introducing them to firearms are two entirely different paths, and that no matter how hard you try you will never be able to be with your child everywhere, all the time.

Young children love to have fun and are usually excited to repeat pleasant, successful activities. Your job is to make sure that happens every time.

HOW TO FORMULATE A LESSON PLAN
(FROM A TEACHER'S PERSPECTIVE)

By Gail Luciano, Educator with more than 30 years of results-oriented, youth teaching experience.

If you were going to construct a building, would you just start nailing together boards? Digging holes? Would you build the roof first and then the floor? How about something simple like planting a garden? Where would it be? How many rows would it have? What vegetables would you plant, and where?

You wish to teach a youth the safe and proper handling of firearms. Where do you begin? You need a plan. Educators call this plan a Lesson Plan.

A lesson plan is a guide, made by the teacher, that covers the subject matter in the area of learning you are trying to teach. It begins with a heading, and then is broken down into the main category, with sub-categories in each of the learning areas. The heading is the subject, the main category is the main objective or learning concept, and the sub-categories list the methods you will use to reach your main objective.

It is much like the outline you would make to create a composition or theme paper. If, for example, you want to teach a Language lesson on verbs: The heading would be Language, the main category would be Verbs, and the sub-categories would be things like:

1. Make a list of things that show action, like running, jumping, talking.
2. Draw a picture to illustrate these actions.
3. Write a sentence to go with your picture, etc.

Teaching students in the primary grades (grades one-five) requires that you design a plan covering all areas of the curriculum such as Reading, Mathematics, Writing skills, Science, etc. Teaching in the intermediate to upper grades (grades six-twelve), requires you to design a plan in your specialty area such as Social Studies. This is much like constructing a building. Primary grades are the foundation, intermediate grades are the walls, and the upper grades put on the roof. The same scenario applies to a lesson plan. The heading is the foundation to build on, the categories help build the walls, and the sub-categories give you a start on the roof. The project is complete when the students understand the lesson.

How does an educator decide what to teach? Most of the curriculum taught is decided by the particular district where you teach. Aside from the subject matter, there are state requirements and certain state standards that must be met.

So, how does a teacher decide what to do and how to do it in order to fulfill all of the requirements and insure that each child in the classroom learns what is necessary? The district supplies you with the headings and most of the main categories. You, as the educator, have to come up with the sub-categories. Sometimes you can find ideas from outside sources, like teaching manuals, reference books, computers or fellow educators. Most of the time, however, you just have to be creative.

Remember Tim? What do you think Tim would have done if he had found a loaded gun in someone's house and had no idea of the safe rules of gun handling? Maybe nothing.

Here's the most important question that I would have you answer: When it comes to your children and their lives and safety, is "maybe" an acceptable answer?

PREPARING TO INTRODUCE A YOUNG CHILD TO GUNS

Before you begin introducing a young child to firearms keep in mind some of the following suggestions.

First, make sure that you are familiar with the rules of safe gun handling

Learning the rules of safe gun handling is a vital part of the process. Everyone looking to introduce young children to firearms should have a level of expertise that allows them the confidence and ability that, so that when it is time to educate young children about firearms and their proper and safe use, it will already be both intuitive and habitual.

Create fun situations to learn

Creating fun situations to learn is imperative when introducing young children to firearms.

Not planning ahead can create frustration for both you and the child. Not only can this complicate the proper introduction of a child to firearms and firearm safety, a negative experience with an initial introduction can follow that child and sour them on other possible learning situations.

Think of everything that you have enjoyed doing over the course of your life. Now, how many of those things had an initial negative experience associated with them? Perhaps some, but most likely not most.

Be consistent

One of the key concepts of successfully introducing young children to firearms is consistency in your method, materials and means of teaching.

If your child responds well to physical activities, you should proceed with a more hands-on approach and maintain that style throughout the lesson plan. In many cases, the materials used with young children are not going to include a great deal of printed or reading material. Most likely you will be doing a great deal of talking while allowing them to explore the proper firearm for someone of their size and stature. The means of teaching is mostly related to the location and plan of action, or lesson plan, in order to ensure all necessary knowledge and skills are taught. The means should make this easily assimilated and well retained.

Deciding to introduce a young child to firearms requires some reflection and a thorough personal assessment. This endeavor you are about to undertake entails a good deal of preparation. We'll review the steps of the planning phase, to help you decide in what manner you can most easily and effectively introduce your young child to firearms.

PERSONAL INTROSPECTION

Some people are great teachers. Many are not. In many cases, children learn better from a person other than their parent due to conflicting messages, rules and even feelings. A disciplinary incident that occurred between you and your child earlier in the day can have a drastic effect on a child's ability to learn and participate. Losing focus is something that also needs to be addressed often with a young child, as a moment of lost focus or misdirected attention when dealing with a firearm can have serious and even deadly consequences.

My children (who all participate and enjoy shooting) have experienced some of their greatest gains in shooting skill while being taught by somebody else. Honestly consider the following questions before you ever begin introducing a young child to shooting and firearms.

Do you enjoy spending time with children?

This is most likely not an issue with your own children but, as a parent myself, I know that there are times when you need to be away from your child and cannot effectively perform with them around. When you are instructing a child on the handling and/or use of a firearm, that simply cannot happen.

Do you have a great deal of patience?

Young children lose focus quite often. A butterfly flying through your lesson area can completely shut down your teaching session and ability for that day. That's okay.

The important thing to remember is that this lesson and introduction is all about the child. If it is not fun for them, or if it goes on for too long a time period, they will not want to participate. And if they do not participate and effectively learn, they will not obtain and retain the necessary knowledge to keep them safe when you may not be with them.

After some serious introspection and reflection, you may realize that it is better to find a skilled mentor to teach your child about guns and gun safety.

Don't feel bad about this. It is quite often that we separate children from their parents in our group lessons. Sometimes staying in the parent/child team puts too many expectations on each participant. That's not fun.

Are you able to repeat the same thing over and over without becoming frustrated?

You may completely understand a concept or lesson the first time it is

When dealing with children, you must be prepared to repeat the same information, sometimes many times in the same lesson.

presented. Children, and especially young children, learn through effective repetition and practice.

It is been my experience that those children learn the most, and most effectively, when that repetition and practice includes a great deal of hands-on activity and fun.

Ideally, you replied yes to these questions.

If you did not, or you have concerns, I urge you to think carefully before proceeding. Better to wait and have the lesson work out properly than to make an error that may at best sour a child's experience, and at worst create an unsafe situation.

ADDRESSING COST

Many people believe that firearms and shooting are very expensive.

KEEP GUN SAFETY SIMPLE FOR CHILDREN

So much revolves around the technical aspects of child gun safety. Kids understand the meaning of rules when put in their perspective. The tried-and-true method is the "laser" rule. I tell kids a laser is constantly pointing out the end of their barrel. Like Star Wars, the laser destroys and cuts through anything it touches.

Scaring gun safety into our kids does not work.

It is important to teach children about guns and correct handling methods without the scare tactic. Some teachers believe painting a vivid picture scares a child into safety. I don't find this to be the case. An explanation of the consequences of poor safety is needed, but without graphic details. We want our children to be comfortable handling a weapon not scared to use it.

– JL Sumpter,
Outdoor and Firearms Writer

There are certainly guns out there that cost a great deal of money. However, the reality is that, with the proper planning and research, you can actually educate young children about firearms and expose them to shooting at a very low cost... even for free.

Dedicating your energy to laying some groundwork prior to the first lesson – learning how children learn, deciding what type of firearm would be best to start with and planning your curriculum – is a good starting point.

I recommend not spending a great deal of money on a bunch of brand-new equipment. You can accomplish a great deal of the education and training to properly introduce your child to firearms with a minimal amount of gear, and much of it can be acquired by borrowing, purchasing on the used firearm and resale market, or even attending an event or visiting a gun store or range where those firearms are located.

Especially in the case of young children, spending a great deal of money will most likely not make your introduction to firearms any more effective. You should use a firearm that fires inexpensive ammunition, does not have any adverse effects like recoil and is easy and rather intuitive to use. The last thing you want is to have to stop early or shoot less because of the cost of ammunition, an aversion to loud noise or the pain of recoil.

Remember, in order to have the greatest success, you want to have more of a plan then waking up one day and saying, "I think I will instill a lifelong love and knowledge of the safe handling of firearms in my child today."

If you plan on doing it yourself, introducing a child to the safe use of handling firearms is more than a simple task that can be checked off. It can be, and most often is, a long-term commitment.

There will be times when you become frustrated. There will be times when the child will become frustrated. When this occurs, take a deep breath, pause what you're doing, evaluate the situation and decide the appropriate action to move forward.

The reality is that these skills will help your child be knowledgeable and, more importantly, remain safe throughout their life. Therefore, the training deserves the proper focus, time and attention.

Most likely, you will experience some benefit as well. Learning the rules of safe gun handling, creating fun situations to learn in, along with being consistent, all involve skills that, once learned, can assist you in other areas of your life.

As an example, for the past 20 or more years I've made a majority of my living as a commissioned sales representative. A large portion of sales involves the education of the customer about the product or service. Teaching skills can certainly transfer between subjects, and even I am surprised by the amount of benefit I have received from spending many hours teaching children about guns.

Obviously, I can't offer my sales prospect an ice cream cone if we find ourselves in a stressful situation, but there are many other techniques – such as rephrasing a question, using an easily understandable analogy, or even drawing a quick diagram – that have had the result of gaining me a large number of accounts and sales over my career.

Patience is also a large component of the sales process, as some prospects that clearly need your product or service (and even may want it) just aren't ready to make that purchase right now.

If this were your prospect, wouldn't you rather earn all of their business moving forward at their preferred pace than force them to move according to your (or, more likely, your boss's) timeline and only getting one sale, or maybe losing their business entirely?

This is of the same importance.

My recommendation to you is to always have a backup plan, even if that backup plan is quickly packing everything up and heading to the nearest ice cream shop for a couple of scoops.

One of the most important things you can do when planning your introduction of the child to firearms is to allow enough time for the lessons you want to teach but not so much time that a child will lose interest or become bored with what you are doing. Most importantly, it has to be F-U-N.

One of the most enjoyable parts of learning safe gun handling is shooting. Make certain that each lesson in your initial stages of introduction allows as much or more actual shooting and other engaging and FUN activities as lesson time.

PLAY, FUN AND LEARNING

There is not specific research that explores the relationship of play, fun and firearm safety and use. Much of the instructions, tips and helpful anecdotes here are a result of my almost four decades of firearm experience and decades of personally instructing thousands of youth. There are, however, many recognized experts in the field of "play" as it applies to a child's learning capacity.

Peter Gray is a PhD research professor at Boston College. His recent book, *Free to Learn: Why Unleashing the Instinct to Play Will Make Our Children Happier, More Self-Reliant, and Better Students for Life,* delves deeply into the relationship between children's play and learning.

In a recent paper, "The decline of play in the rise in psychopathology in children and adolescents" (American Journal of Play, volume three, number 4, p. 443), he reviews research on the restriction of play in childhood and values of children being allowed to play.

There are several startling conclusions based on the review of the research but, mainly, "play functions as the major means by which children: 1. Develop intrinsic interest and competencies; 2. Learn how to make decisions, solve problems, exert self-control, and follow rules; 3. Learn to regulate their emotions; 4. Make friends and learn to get along with others as equals; and, 5. Experience joy. Through all of these effects, play promotes mental health."

Laurel Bongiorno, PhD, is the director of Champlain College's graduate program in early childhood education, with specializations in teaching and administration, in Burlington, Vermont. She has taught preschool, directed early childhood programs, and studied parents' perceptions of preschoolers' learning through play. Following is her list of "10 Things Every Parent Should Know About Play."

1. Children learn through their play.

Don't underestimate the value of play. Children learn and develop:
- Cognitive skills – like math and problem solving in a pretend grocery store
- Physical abilities – like balancing blocks and running on the playground
- New vocabulary – like the words they need to play with toy dinosaurs
- Social skills – like playing together in a pretend car wash
- Literacy skills – like creating a menu for a pretend restaurant

2. Play is healthy.

Play helps children grow strong and healthy. It also counteracts obesity issues facing many children today.

3. Play reduces stress.

Play helps your children grow emotionally. It is joyful and provides an outlet for anxiety and stress.

4. Play is more than meets the eye.

Play is simple and complex. There are many types of play: symbolic, socio-dramatic, functional and games with rules—to name just a few. Researchers study play's many aspects: how children learn through play, how outdoor play impacts children's health, the effects of screen time on play, to the need for recess in the school day.

5. Make time for play.

As parents, you are the biggest supporters of your children's learning. You can make sure they have as much time to play as possible during the day to promote cognitive, language, physical, social and emotional development.

6. Play and learning go hand-in-hand.

They are not separate activities. They are intertwined. Think about them as a science lecture with a lab. Play is the child's lab.

7. Play outside.

Remember your own outdoor experiences of building forts, playing on the beach, sledding in the winter or playing with other children in the neighborhood. Make sure your children create outdoor memories too.

8. There's a lot to learn about play.

There's a lot written on children and play. David Elkind's *The Power of Play* (Da Capo, 2007 reprint) is also a great resource.

9. Trust your own playful instincts.

Remember as a child how play just came naturally? Give your children time for play and see all that they are capable of when given the opportunity.

10. Play is a child's context for learning.

Children practice and reinforce their learning in multiple areas during play. It gives them a place and a time for learning that cannot be achieved through completing a worksheet. For example, in playing restaurant, children write and draw menus, set prices, take orders and make out checks. Play provides rich learning opportunities and leads to children's success and self-esteem.

(Source: http://families.naeyc.org/learning-and-development/child-development/10-things-every-parent-should-know-about-play#sthash.f0PQd-9wp.dpuf)

Finally, Dr. Alison Gopnik is the professor of psychology and an affiliate professor of philosophy at the University of California Berkeley. She has completed numerous studies of children that demonstrate children are intellectually more skilled and more advanced in their thinking than previously believed.

It is her belief that, "one area that has been overlooked this outdoor play. Outdoor play needs to do more than just offer children opportunities for physical exercise. Children also need opportunities to explore. They need places to investigate. They need stairs to climb and they need trees to hide behind. They need to have a sense that they are discovering something new going on around them."

In addition, she believes that children of preschool age are much more open and that the things that they get to explore during this time can be of most importance later on.

"Preschool is a part of a great evolutionary story. The preschool years may be the most important time of learning we ever have. The preschool years, from an evolutionary point of view, are an extended period of immaturity in human lifespan. But it is during this period of immaturity the exploration and play take place. Ultimately, exploration and play during preschool turns us into adults who are flexible and sophisticated thinkers. If you look across the animal kingdom, you'll find that the more flexible the adult is, the longer that animal has had a chance to be immature.

"I think that even the term preschooler is a bit misleading… It implies that our job is to get children ready for school and that school is where the important things happen. But rreschool isn't just about readiness. It's an important entity in its own right. Indeed, what preschool teachers do is arguably more important than what occurs in the elementary school. And I think we have lots and lots of evidence of that now." (from http://www.naeyc.org/files/tyc/file/TYC_V3N2_Gopnik.pdf)

What is evident from these experts in child learning is that young children are more open to learning at this period of their life than at any other. Conclusion: This is an excellent time to build lifetime awareness of the possible danger of misusing a firearm, habits like proper handling and safety, and enjoyable experiences that can translate to lifelong passions, should that be your goal.

There is a large body of evidence supporting that children learn and learn best through play. Conclusion: Play is fun and experientially-oriented, therefore, the more fun and experience-oriented you can make your introduction of firearms to a young child, the greater success you will have.

Young depends on the child, not a specific age. Conclusion: A young child can be an ideal student of lifetime lessons, provided the education is presented the right way.

Outdoor play is an essential part of a child's development. Conclusion: The preferred introduction of young children to firearms should take place in an open, outdoor environment.

Fun is important, but just as important is understanding how your child prefers to learn.

DETERMINING LEARNING TYPE

It is generally agreed that children can be divided into three different types of learning styles. Those three styles are visual, auditory and kinesthetic.

Children who are visual learners rely mostly on their sight and observation. They will generally prefer to see things in written form, quite often they use things such as pictures, graphical representations, and other types of visual learning tools. Overall, most young people remember things better by seeing something written.

If you are teaching a youth that is a visual learner, an excellent and helpful tool to have with you is a notebook and pen or even a small dry erase board for doing things like drawing proper sight alignment, using descriptive words and writing important things like the four cardinal rules of gun safety so that they can be seen.

Youth who are more auditory in their learning retain knowledge best by listening. They prefer to have things demonstrated, watching videos, observing someone speaking and engaging in discussions. These youth will remember things best through hearing things and, even more so, by saying and repeating things themselves.

A kinesthetic learner is someone who learns best touching, feeling and having a more physical experience in the area in which they are striving to learn. These children will remember best by writing things down, physically handling, touching and demonstrating with the firearm, and by doing interactive activities like role-plays and active practice.

You want to identify what type of learner you have by both effective questioning and observation. Watch your children carefully and note some of their preferred behaviors.

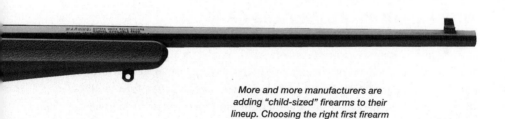

More and more manufacturers are adding "child-sized" firearms to their lineup. Choosing the right first firearm is about what works and what fits.

Most visual learners are observed spending time doodling, drawing, and manipulating graphical representations, and are drawn to picture, computer-driven or video Learning experiences.

Many auditory learners will speak aloud to themselves and read things that they are trying to learn out loud, therefore enhancing their retention of the information.

A kinesthetic learner will often prefer to learn things by writing them down, or taking an active part. You may observe them taking notes on things regardless of whether or not they refer to them later on. They also tend to try and figure things out rather than reading through long and tedious directions.

RECOMMENDED FIREARMS FOR YOUNG CHILDREN

My recommendations for introducing a young child to firearms is a youth-sized, lead pellet-firing, medium velocity air rifle or a special youth-sized, single-shot .22-caliber rifle similar to offerings from Cricket Firearms and Savage's "Rascal" line and, more specifically, using the air rifle first, and then graduating to the .22.

The reason for this is threefold:

A medium velocity air rifle and a "micro" sized .22 are still powerful enough to use for the demonstration of power described later in chapter 10, giving hands-on opportunity to learn how dangerous a firearm can be if used improperly.

An air rifle may be effectively used at home, both inside and outside, allowing for more frequent opportunity for both participation and learning – something demonstrated as important in young children's ability to learn.

Ammunition for both is very inexpensive, so your child can participate as much and as long as they want without you worrying about affordability.

BEFORE YOU START YOUR INSTRUCTION
WITH FIREARMS, REGARDLESS OF AGE...

It is an undisputed fact that we live in a right-handed world. If you have any doubts, just pick up any pair of scissors out there and try to cut with them left-handed. We are such a right-hand dominant society that we even drive on the right side of the road. The vast majority of Americans and, therefore, children that you will have the opportunity to introduce to firearms will be right-handed.

Some won't be.

For left-handed shooters, the good news is that there are now more options than ever for them in bolt-action and semi-automatic firearm choices. The bad news is that the options are still rather limited, and most often call him at a slightly premium cost due to their much lower sales volume compared to right-handed firearms.

The best news? When dealing strictly with an introduction to firearms, quite often the difference will be negligible and rather easy to overcome.

Fortunately, most rifle and shotgun stocks made and sold in the United States are of a straight design. That is, there is no cast (a degree of offset to the left or right side from a straight line to more easily align the proper sight picture) that would further complicate the ability to obtain a good sight picture with a weapon.

Therefore, if a left-handed child needs to use a right-handed firearm, they will be able to acquire the proper sight alignment with no more or less effort than their right-handed counterparts.

Here are some tips to avoid frustration should you have a left-handed shooter.

Buy or borrow a left-handed firearm

When shooting a semi-automatic long gun such as a shotgun or rifle, the largest inconvenience to the left-handed shooter is that the empty cartridges will eject from the right side across their body and more in their view than a right-handed shooter firing the same firearm. This issue is also the case with almost every semi-automatic handgun out there. For a left-handed shooter, a revolver eliminates this problem.

When firing a bolt-action rifle, however, there is the added complication of

Notice that the bolt of the rifle action is opposite the hand that is supposed to work the action.

the bolt handle being opposite the side of their free hand.

In order to work/cycle the action on a right-handed, bolt-action rifle, someone shooting left-handed is required to reach back towards themselves to lift the
bolt handle on the right side, cycle it back and forth, push it back down into the
locked position, and then move the strong hand over and around the gun stock
to reach the grip and trigger area. This creates a great deal of extra motion and
work, but I have seen left-handed shooters who have shot right-handed, bolt-
action rifles their entire lives conquer this challenge very, very rapidly. Ideally,
a left-handed person should shoot a bolt-action firearm that has the bolt on the
left side of the gun.

An additional concern with left-handed shooters is that the safety mechanism on right-handed firearms is, appropriately, located on the right side. For a
lefty, that is backwards.

Left-handed firearms have the safety located to be operated from left to right
or ambidextrously on the rear of the firearm action above the grip.

*An over/under shotgun can eliminate the issue of a left-handed shooter having to shoot a right-
handed gun.*

Use an over/under or single-shot shotgun, or buy a Browning BPS

Over/under and single-shot shotguns have no ejection port that throws out an empty hull. To remove the empty case, the gun must be opened and the cartridge(s) are either manually removed by pulling them out with your fingers, or ejected out by a spring-loaded ejection mechanism.

In addition, the safety is located on the top of the grip area, immediately to the rear of the action, rendering it ambidextrous.

The Browning BPS is unique in that it ejects all empty cartridges to the bottom of the firearm (an advantage when cleaning up!) and contains the safety mechanism on top of the grip, immediately to the rear of the action, similar to an over/under or single-shot. (Note: the Ithaca model 37 also is a bottom-ejecting shotgun, if you can find one. They have stopped and started production numerous times over the years.)

Note: I am not a fan of single-shot, exposed hammer shotguns. More about that in Chapter 9, choosing the right gear.

Buy a right-handed firearm and pay a gunsmith to reverse the safety

Sometimes, you can find such great deals on used, youth-sized firearms that it may be worth your while to buy a firearm that fits your child and pay a gunsmith to reverse the safety – a simple process making the safety located to the front or rear of the trigger guard turn on and off by pushing from the left side to the right, rather than from the right to the left. This is often only a minor inconvenience, but correcting it is something that enhances safety and that I recommend.

DETERMINING EYE DOMINANCE

The proper and effective use of a firearm requires the use of your entire body, and one of the most important body parts used in shooting is your eyes. After all, we can't shoot what we can't see!

In addition, and with the only exceptions being the use of a laser or telescopic sight (something that is not recommended for introduction to firearms), your child will need to be able to properly align the front and rear sights, or in the case of a shotgun be able to properly sight along the top of the barrel and see the front bead.

Because of this, knowing which is their dominant eye is essential.

Just as most people are right-hand or left-hand dominant, almost everyone will have a dominant eye that they use more often, even though we all have bifocal vision. One of the ways to determine both hand and eye dominance is a quick, simple game that also includes a fun safety lesson.

Remember, we never, ever, ever point a gun at anything we do not want to shoot or kill. The only exception to that rule is the "finger gun."

I make my own finger gun and pretend to have it holstered at my side.

Then I shout, "Draw," and have them aim their fingers at me.

This does two things almost immediately. First, a child will almost always use their dominant hand to perform this exercise (but not always). Second, by standing in front of them I can most often determine which eye is their dominant eye.

The majority of the time I will have a child or a group of children pointing at me with their right hand and either have their left eye closed or at least sighting their finger gun at me with their right eye. Some will have their left hands out, sighting with their left eye.

Then, there are the select few…

WHAT IS "CROSS EYE DOMINANCE"?

Cross eye dominance is when someone has the opposite dominant eye to their dominant hand.

This occurs when a right-handed person is left-eye dominant, or a left-handed person is right-eye dominant. These children will most often be easy to spot, as during the finger gun test they will have their right

Most children will aim their finger gun with their dominant hand and their dominant eye.

hand out but be clearly aiming with their left eye. If they try to am a long gun, such as a rifle, most often they will bring the gun up to their right side and try to put their left cheek on the stock or at least turn their head to the right to use their left eye (and opposite if left-handed).

You will want to further evaluate these children with a more specific test of eye dominance to verify your observations. To do so, have the child reach out with both hands in front of them and create a window using their index finger and thumb approximately two inches across. Then, choose an object for them to center in that window with both eyes open.

Ask the child to not move their head or hands at all and to close what you believe to be their non-dominant eye. The object should still be viewable to them inside their window if that is, in fact, their dominant eye.

Next, to confirm eye dominance, have them open their closed eye, sight at the same object, the same way, with both eyes open and then close their dominant eye. The object should move out of their sight.

In young children, you will most often see them move their head or hands at this point in order to regain their sight picture. Older children should be able to tell you that the object has moved.

By making a "window" with their hands and focusing on an object, you can confirm which is a child's dominant eye.

If the child is, in fact, cross eye dominant, you will have a few challenges to deal with right away.

DEALING WITH CROSS EYE DOMINANCE

If you have a child that is cross eye dominant, there are two ways that you can handle their introduction of firearms.

1) Have them shoot with their dominant eye rather than their dominant hand.

This means that a right-handed shooter that is left-eye dominant will shoot left-handed, and a left-handed shooter that is right-eye dominant will learn to shoot right-handed.

Fortunately, if this is an initial introduction, the child will likely adapt to the initial, not as comfortable position with it becoming easier in each successive session. If they are unable to adapt easily, you may want to train their non-dominant eye.

2) Train their non-dominant eye.

Have the child shoot with one eye open or, preferably, use a piece of tape on the dominant eye side of their shooting protection to obscure the vision in the dominant eye.

This is the preferred method for introduction. With safety being the number one concern, it is easier for a child to maintain control of a firearm with their dominant hand being used.

THE "EDDIE EAGLE PROGRAM"

For young children, I highly recommend the Eddie Eagle program. This effective education tool can be introduced in a non-threatening situation and specifically doesn't even include guns in the criteria. From the NRA Eddie Eagle program website:

The NRA Eddie Eagle Program

The Eddie Eagle GunSafe® Program teaches children in pre-K through third grade four important steps to take if they find a gun. These steps are presented by the program's mascot, Eddie Eagle, in an easy-to-remember format consisting of the following simple rules:

If you see a gun:

STOP!

Don't Touch.

Leave the Area.

Tell an Adult.

Begun in 1988, The Eddie Eagle GunSafe® Program has reached more than 26 million children - in all 50 states. This program was developed through the combined efforts of such qualified professionals as clinical psychologists, reading specialists, teachers, curriculum specialists, urban housing safety officials, and law enforcement personnel.

Anyone may teach The Eddie Eagle GunSafe® Program, and NRA membership is not required. The program may be readily incorporated into existing school curriculum, taught in a one- to five-day format, and used to reach both levels or simply one or two grades. Materials available through this program are: student workbooks, seven-minute animated DVD, instructor guides, brochures, and student reward stickers. Program materials are also available in Spanish.

The NRA is committed to helping keep America's young children safe. In efforts to do so, we offer our program at a nominal fee. Schools, law enforcement agencies, hospitals, daycare centers, and libraries may be eligible to receive grant funding to defray program costs. Grant funding is available in many states to these groups to cover the cost of all program curriculum materials.

The purpose of the Eddie Eagle Program isn't to teach whether guns are good or bad, but rather to promote the protection and safety of children. The program makes no value judgments about firearms, and no firearms are ever used in the program. Like swimming pools, electrical outlets, matchbooks and household poison, they're treated simply as a fact of everyday life. With firearms found in about half of all American households, it's a stance that makes sense.

Eddie Eagle is never shown touching a firearm, and he does not promote firearm ownership or use. The program prohibits the use of Eddie Eagle mascots anywhere that guns are present. The Eddie Eagle Program has no agenda other than accident prevention - ensuring that children stay safe should they encounter a gun. The program never mentions the NRA. Nor does it encourage children to buy guns or to become NRA members. The NRA does not receive any appropriations from Congress, nor is it a trade organization. It is not affiliated with any firearm or ammunition manufacturers or with any businesses that deal in guns and ammunition.

CHAPTER FOUR

Tweens
and Guns

©National Shooting Sports Foundation, Inc.

Official definitions vary slightly, but for the purposes of this book, a tween is, a person who is between the ages of 10 and 12 years old. The term is often described in popular media as a preadolescent who is at the "in-between" stage in their development. Tweens are at a crossroads in their lives.

They still retain a great deal of the openness and innocence of their younger years, and have not quite yet experienced the hormonal surge that can lead to emotional outbursts, conflicts, becoming argumentative, and, perhaps most importantly, developing a significant interest in members of the opposite sex.

According to all of the experts in child psychology, education and scientific world, every child learns in a slightly different way. The short version is that every kid is different, even tweens. As described in Chapter 3, figuring out that individual learning style will be the key to your success.

It is not likely that you will have insurmountable obstacles when introducing a tween to firearms. However, as we saw, there are certain things about children's learning behavior that may help you avoid frustration on both sides.

If the child is your own, you will know much about them. Complications may arise when you're introducing one of their friends or, perhaps a youth who you don't know, to something that requires a great deal of attention and needs to be handled with a great deal of responsibility – in this case a gun.

The good news is that most children have fully developed their learning style by the time they hit the tween stage, and if you have properly evaluated them, you will know how to teach them.

MYTH: 12 YEARS OLD IS THE PROPER AGE TO INTRODUCE CHILDREN TO GUNS

The truth is, the proper age to introduce a child to firearm SAFETY is from three to four years old. By that age, a child has a basic understanding of right and wrong, yes and no, and, most importantly, pain and danger.

You will recall from Chapter 3 that I recommend the Eddie Eagle program for all young children, but the safety message in that program translates to all ages.

The proper age to introduce a child to FIREARMS is… whatever age you deem appropriate, based upon your experience, knowledge, comfort, teaching ability and patience; your extended and careful observation of the child's maturity and ability to understand the essential concepts of safety; and the child's physical ability to safely handle the firearm.

The short answer: The proper age to introduce a child to firearms depends on the child.

Ask yourself (or, the parents of the child you are teaching) questions that will help you anticipate any challenges that may arise. Does the child have any learning issues? Are they labeled with a condition such as attention deficit disorder (ADD) or attention deficit hyperactivity disorder (ADHD)? Do they tend to learn better hands-on, or do they work best through language and do well with reading things first and then putting it into practice? If this is the case, they are probably relatively good students in school, because the overwhelming method of teaching is, "read, answer questions and listen to the teacher."

If you hand kinetic learners a booklet and tell them to read it and answer questions before you start something more enjoyable, you may run into trouble.

Conversely, if you try to bring up a child of the tween ages to use as an example in something that they have little to no knowledge about, their embarrassment can complicate their ability to learn. I have seen brilliant, dynamic children unable to speak and function when brought up in front of their peers.

Tweens are rapid learners, and the author's experience has been that tween girls tend to be easier to teach than tween boys.

UNIQUE ASPECTS OF TWEENS

You might find this hard to believe, but if I had to pick a preferred age and gender to introduce to firearms, it would be the female tween. It is been my experience, and, the experience of hundreds of other youth mentors and instructors that I have spoken to, that females, in general, are easier to teach firearm safety and use. They tend to be overall less aggressive, less know-it-all and more open to instruction at just about every level. It is certainly something you should consider when teaching a youth/child about firearms and firearm safety.

Tweens are at the stage of their life when they assimilate knowledge rapidly. Their brain is in a highly active developmental state, and it is specifically at this time in their lives that they develop and exhibit habits, patterns and passions that will follow them for the rest of their lives.

I find it is much easier to introduce a youth of this age to firearms and have them develop a passion for firearms, rather than wait until later in their life when they have already established preferred hobbies and recreation. Your experience may be different, but it is certainly something to consider.

Also, youth at this age are deciding what they want to do in school, sports and life in general, and you may fill a void in their lives by helping them experience shooting.

The other side of this coin is that this is when many youth become extremely busy with other activities. Think of the people you know that have children of this age. They tend to be running around between school, play, soccer, karate, baseball, hockey, glee club, tutoring, basketball… you get the point.

You will be competing with every other activity that a child of this age is involved in, and today that can mean a lot. Plus, tweens that are involved in competitive sports tend to be much more competitive and committed to their sport of choice than, say, your average seven-year-old.

An example: I was an active baseball player in my youth that qualified for many of the traveling teams in our area. We practiced twice a week, played 12 regular-season games and 16-20 travel games from May to September, and I still had quite a bit of time to shoot over the summer.

Now, I know several different parents whose children belong to an adolescent traveling baseball team in a northern-tier state that begins the season in January!

This is not to say that a child who is very active in sports will not have time or desire to participate in shooting sports. As a matter of fact, it is often quite the contrary. These children experience shooting, most likely find it enjoyable, but as they move "onward and upward" in their sport they find less and less time to participate in multiple activities. They put shooting aside for the most part, but then, when their career in sports is over, find that they want to participate in something active and sometimes even competitive as they grow up.

My own son became heavily involved in hockey as a youngster, eventually making the cut to play for a Junior-level hockey team (a level between high school and professional hockey). His season, even as a 14-year-old, went from October to April, with additional training and drills beginning in August. Conversely, his participation in hunting was limited to a few times per year and, as he got older, to almost none at all. Now, as a young adult in his twenties, he has bought his own firearms and shoots recreationally as well as hunts with us again.

A lot of kids also start dropping out of sports in big numbers at the tween stage. Playing sports loses its enjoyment for them and the fun they experienced in recreational leagues and organizations takes a back seat to winning. Pick-up games and just playing for fun that should be encouraged usually are not. The key at this vulnerable stage is to keep kids playing the sports they enjoy, and if you've already had some fun introductory sessions with them at the range before this occurs, one of those sports could be shooting. Not being on a team at this age does not mean that they have failed as athletes. It just means that they are looking to find other pleasurable ways to continue enjoying sports.

Here is where shooting and firearms can really shine. Let's use Tim, my son's friend referenced in the beginning of this book. Tim was physically challenged. I've taught dozens of kids with challenges like Tim, as well as kids in wheelchairs, kids with Attention Deficit Disorder, kids who were the strongest and biggest in their class, and kids who were the smallest and weakest.

There is a famous saying that "God created man, but Sam Colt made them equal." I once watched an elite hockey player get absolutely schooled on the trap range by a wheelchair-bound girl (in his defense, she was an elite-level shooter).

It also means that, due to an almost unlimited array of options open to them, you need to catch their attention immediately. Over the course of an afternoon, a child can be faced with simple choices like, "Do I want a burger or a hot dog? Should I play angry birds right now or Jetpack Joyride? iPad or iPhone?" They also face more complex choices, like, "Which of the 200+ television channels should I watch? Should I DVR all three shows and watch one, or watch a different one and watch those three later? Then should I ride my bike or play my Xbox?"

That is just a small sample of one day that you'll be competing with. So, how do you determine the steps you should take when introducing a tween to firearms, their use and safety?

INTRODUCING FIREARMS TO TWEENS

As with all proper introductions, the very first thing you should discuss is safety. The parts and mechanisms of the weapon and the "dangerous end" compared to the "safe end" should be discussed at the beginning of every session with every level of youth that you introduce.

With a tween, it's all about the "wow" factor and grabbing their attention immediately. Not as content to punch holes in paper as a younger child might be, you may need to introduce a reactive target to hold their attention. With tweens I will often add a little surprise by using an exploding target, such as Tannerite.

Many tweens will already have a basic knowledge and interest in guns. Most have experienced video games, a great deal of which are of the "first–person shooter" variety. This can be of great benefit or detriment, and depends on the child. (We more thoroughly examine video games and their effects on kids and guns in Chapter 6.)

After our speech on safety and the importance of immediate obedience of any and all instructions while on the range, I always start an introduction of firearms to youth with the demonstration of power.

It gets the point across rather well, and shows them immediately that no matter what type of weapon you are using it has great destructive power. (For how to set up the demonstration of power, refer to Chapter 10.)

With tweens, you may need to introduce a reactive target to hold their attention.

I believe it is always good to relate what you are doing to things that are relevant and pertinent to the child, their social group, and their background/demographic. That can mean a different approach in instruction between a group of urban kids and rural kids.

Why is that? For the most part, rural kids tend to have a much greater familiarity with firearms and what they are used for. Usually someone in their network of family or friends has guns, uses guns, hunts, shoots or uses a gun to protect livestock from predators like coyotes. Those kids require a much different instruction than a child who has grown up thinking that "country" means an open space of greater than five acres.

Following are the steps I use in introducing tweens to firearms.

1. Do something exciting right away to captivate their attention. This can be something as simple as shooting a soda can of water. Tannerite works well with this crowd, and better if it is a complete surprise.

2. Whenever possible, I use reactive targets with tweens, as I find they become bored easily with shooting paper. Some of my favorites are clay pigeons or small balloons staked out on a string in the wind. If reactive targets are

The tween stage can be a good time to introduce competition.

unavailable or not allowed, I find that some of the new Zombie targets that have a color change when shot can make things more interesting.

3. Play the "video game" card. Earlier we mentioned that many tweens have first-person-shooter-type gaming experience. Being a parent who has experienced a decade of tween issues, interests and activities, I can usually come up with some references to relevant or at least familiar games with which youths I am instructing can relate.

4. Introduce competition. Tweens, especially male tweens, are in a constant state of competition. They compete for attention, they compete in sports and they compete for social status. Remember, shooting is a level playing field. It is often exciting to see the small outshoot the large, the girl outshoot the boy, etc. If you are only working with one child, use prior target scores, reactive target hits per session, etc. to establish competition against previous performance. We will discuss competition more extensively in Chapter 14.

RECOMMENDED FIREARMS FOR TWEENS

Full power, full-sized air rifles
20-gauge shotguns, preferably semi-automatic
Full-sized .22-caliber rifles
I do not recommend handguns for an introduction to firearms at this age.

MYTH: A .410 IS AN EXCELLENT FIRST SHOTGUN FOR A YOUTH

At best, a .410 is a good caliber (the .410 is a bore diameter, rather than a gauge determination) for an initial introduction to the concept of a shotgun for a smaller-framed shooter, and then at stationary targets only. It has the advantages of light weight and low recoil, sometimes referred to as "kick." (By the way, try not to use this highly negative connotation when describing recoil. Would you like to be 'kicked"?)

But, the .410 is actually a "shooter's shotgun." That is, it gives several large handicaps to the shooter in the form of substantially less shot (meaning it is harder to hit a moving target with it, as shotguns are designed to do), and it's generally light weight decreases the inertia when swinging through a moving target, tending to stop the shooter's swing and resulting in a missed target.

A much better choice for a young shooter is a youth-sized, semi-automatic 20-gauge. The semi-automatic action uses some of the firearm's recoil to cycle the action, and you can get light, low-recoil loads for introduction and practice, as well as heavier, more energy-producing loads for target games or hunting.

CHAPTER FIVE

Teens and Guns

©National Shooting Sports Foundation, Inc.

"Our youth now love luxury. They have bad manners, contempt for authority; they show disrespect for their elders and love chatter in place of exercise; they no longer rise when elders enter the room; they contradict their parents, chatter before company; gobble up their food and tyrannize their teachers." -Socrates

Though we as parents and teachers would like to believe we are the first to deal with teenagers and their associated "-isms" and issues, it would appear that not a lot has changed regarding the teenage attitude over the past 2500 or so years.

They are pushed up between childhood and adulthood over a five- or six-year period where they, for the most part, are adult in size and stature yet retain youthful levels of maturity.

It used to be relatively uncommon that introduction to firearms began in the

Teens have a lot going on, but there is usually a division between "serious" teens and those who have not yet reached a mature level when it comes to things like guns.

teen years. However, as the incidence of single parent and divided households has grown, there has been a decided increase in the number of teens having their first experience with guns in junior high and high school.

In addition, the prevalence of the Scholastic Clay Target Program gives many teens who have not had the opportunity to experience shooting or shooting sports at home an introduction through friends and high school coaches.

It has been my observation that most teens' desire to experience firearms and shooting is driven by the teen independent of, but not necessarily without, the support of their parents. There are several types of teens that I have found to most often seek firearms exposure and instruction.

1. The mature teen. These teens have most likely sought out exposure and

Many teens with little to no experience want to learn guns for the "cool factor."

experience on their own, and for many different reasons. Perhaps they have previously been busy with other sports and athletics. Most likely, they will come because of an innate curiosity about guns and their use.

2. The young teen with no mentors. This is usually a child who has some type of connection to firearms, but is once-removed. Perhaps they have a close friend that hunts and shoots. Maybe they have a desire to try one of the relatively new Scholastic Shooting programs and not feel inadequate. Even though these programs are very well run and I have never heard of anything but the most accepting of attitudes and opinions, peer pressure is a big deal with teens. In this case, they may seek out knowledge so that they seem "firearm smart" when with their friends.

3. The active gamer. The prevalence of the first-person shooter games and their vast social followings has given both a good and bad introduction of firearms to teens. Yes, it is somewhat refreshing for a child to know the difference between a rifle, a shotgun, and a handgun, but the method of introduction is what concerns me.

More and more of our children are playing these games for a greater and greater amount of time. I am simply not comfortable with the idea of an increasingly realistic-looking firearm and sight picture pointed at and actually shooting and killing people – albeit virtually – being not simply encouraged, but exalted by such a peer group-dominated activity. (More on video games and their effects in Chapter 6.)

Additionally, I find these active gamers tend to come for two reasons: curiosity and cool factor.

Teens in the "cool factor" camp need to be monitored a bit more carefully and, certainly, if I hear discussion about things like "damage" or "blow people away," my hackles rise a bit.

Regardless of your opinion about games, you need to make certain that a teen is properly introduced to respect for firearms, the safe handling of firearms, and can recite the four cardinal rules of firearm safety before you ever allow them to handle a loaded weapon.

There is good news regarding this group of teens: You can keep them engaged and riveted throughout your introductory lessons by showing them an AR-style firearm (even if it's a .22-caliber) with the promise of shooting it as soon as they pass the beginning lessons.

UNIQUE ASPECTS OF TEENS

According to a recent, random survey of over 6400 teens nationwide by StageOfLife.com, our teenagers deal with a multitude of issues, but there are several that clearly stand out.

The top three things that gave teens the most difficulty this past school year (along with the percentage of teens citing that issue as the biggest problem) were:

• School-related issues (bullying, teachers, homework, graduation): 27%
• Self image: 20%
• Parents: 16%

Other categories such as friends, drugs and alcohol, siblings, boy/girlfriends, etc. fell further down the list, but can have a distinct and profound effect on your introduction of a teen to firearms. (From http://www.stageoflife.com/Teen_Challenges.aspx)

How will this affect your introduction of a teen to firearms? In several ways.

Distractions are never a good thing when teaching firearms, and all of these issues fall into that category. School pressure, peer pressure, parent pressure, boyfriend/girlfriend pressure can cause a teen to zone out when they should be listening to instructions.

This should always be at the forefront of your mind, as it is your job to maintain focus and interest such that your students are able to not only observe, but to retain and repeat what you are teaching.

This brings up another excellent point…

CELL PHONES AND FIREARMS

Most schools prohibit the use of cellular phones while class is in session. Some even require that personal phones be "checked in" when class starts and "checked out" at the end of class.

They do this because today's smart phones are able to find answers in seconds rather than requiring the proper study and thought. The teachers want to make certain that the students maintain the proper focus in class, learn the materials and retain the knowledge that participation allows.

When introducing a youth to firearms, these reasons are also very important.

There is one difference between the school classroom and your firearms classroom.

Not paying attention in English or History can be cause for embarrassment if called upon and the student does not know the answer.

In our classroom, a lack of proper knowledge can mean that somebody dies.

Keep the phones off and put away until after your teaching and shooting session is over.

CHAPTER SIX

How Video Games Can Help - And Hurt

One day, not too long ago I woke up and came to a startling realization… that I am getting old, and with that age comes a degree of yearning for the days of my youth.

The array of entertainment options available to our children today is completely mind-boggling. There are so many choices that simple choosing an activity can occupy a great deal of a child's time. We certainly didn't have that problem.

If it was at all reasonable weather outside (meaning that if left to our own devices we were unlikely to freeze to death, contract heatstroke), we were expected to be outside and occupying ourselves. Indoor activities were rather limited, as cable television was new and novel, and it was a rare home that had it. I believe we were rather fortunate to live within a reasonable distance to a larger metropolitan area in that we had as many as 10 different television channels, depending on the weather. When forced indoors by weather or darkness, we needed a means to entertain ourselves.

As a child, board games were a large and important source of entertainment for my family, but none so much as checkers and chess.

It has always been thought that chess was a "Thinking Man's Game." Benjamin Franklin said, in "The Morals of Chess" (1779): "We learn by chess the habit of not being discouraged by present appearances in the state of our affairs, the habit of hoping for a favorable change, and that of persevering in the search of resources. The game is so full of events, there is such a variety of turns in it, the fortune of it is so subject to sudden vicissitudes, and one so frequently, after long contemplation, discovers the means of extricating one's self from a supposed insurmountable difficulty, that one is encouraged to continue the contest to the last, in hopes of victory from our own skill, or at least of getting a

Chess required planning, forethought, patience and strategy - much like today's video games.

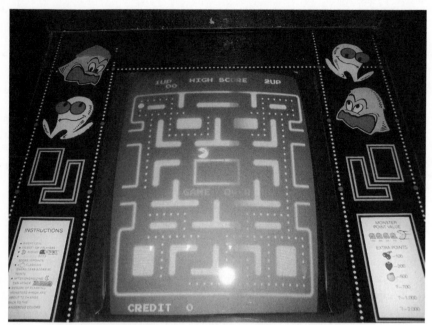
Video games used to be rather simple compared to today, and you had to go to an arcade to play them.

stalemate from the negligence of our adversary . . ."

What was chess back then? Very simply, it was an enjoyable recreational pastime/game that required planning, forethought, patience and strategy that was played by a large number of people in the country. Does anything about that sound familiar?

Now, way back when I was a child, there was an amazing and wondrous device that was introduced to the world. It was called a "video game" and you had to go someplace called an "arcade" that had a bunch of them together in one room that was a cacophony of sounds, sugar-hyped youth and flashing lights, and they required you to stuff quarters into them in order to play.

Not too long after that, a home-based game was introduced – the Atari 2600. It was not fancy by today's standards, but with games like "Space Invaders," "Pong," "Asteroids" and "Tank," they were highly addictive to my generation's youth.

I feel fortunate, now, that my parents did not deign to own any of these devices, and many of my friends' parents felt similarly. Unfortunately, childhood has been drastically altered since. Video games (and especially first-person shooter games) have become today's chess.

There are also those (sometimes including me) who believe that video games are a detriment to the development of a child. As with all things in life, it is likely the case that moderation is key. As for the effects video games can have on introducing a child to firearms, they have their positives and their negatives.

VIDEO GAMES ARE GOOD FOR YOUR CHILD

At least in several areas, according to a study published in "American Psychologist," the journal of the American Psychological Association (APA), in January of 2014. It concludes: "Playing video games, including violent shooter games, may boost children's learning, health and social skills."

The study comes out as debate continues among psychologists and other health professionals regarding the effects of violent media on youth. An APA task force is conducting a comprehensive review of research on violence in video games and interactive media and will release its findings later this year.

"Important research has already been conducted for decades on the negative effects of gaming, including addiction, depression and aggression, and we are certainly not suggesting that this should be ignored," says Isabela Granic, PhD, of Radboud University Nijmegen in The Netherlands, lead author of the article. "However, to understand the impact of video games on children's and adolescents' development, a more balanced perspective is needed.

"While one widely held view maintains that playing video games is intellectually lazy, such play actually may strengthen a range of cognitive skills such as spatial navigation, reasoning, memory and perception, (emphasis mine) according to several studies reviewed in the article. This is particularly true for shooter video games, which are often violent, the authors found. A 2013 meta-analysis found that playing shooter video games improved a player's capacity to think about objects in three dimensions just as well as academic courses designed to enhance these same skills, according to the study." (emphasis mine)

"This has critical implications for education and career development, as previous research has established the power of spatial skills for achievement in science, technology, engineering and mathematics," Granic says.

This enhanced thinking was not found when playing other types of video games, such as puzzles or role-playing games.

Playing video games may also help children develop problem-solving skills, the authors said. The more adolescents reported playing strategic video games, such as role-playing games, the more they improved in problem solving and school grades the following year, according to a long-term study published in 2013. Children's creativity was also enhanced by playing any kind of video game, including violent games, but not when the children used other forms of technology, such as a computer or cell phone, other research revealed.

Simple games that are easy to access and can be played quickly, such as "Angry Birds," can improve players' moods, promote relaxation and ward off anxiety, the study said. "If playing video games simply makes people happier, this seems to be a fundamental emotional benefit to consider," said Granic. The authors also highlighted the possibility that video games are effective tools for learning resilience in the face of failure. By learning to cope with ongoing failures in games, the authors suggest that children build emotional resilience they can rely upon in their everyday lives.

Another stereotype the research challenges is the socially isolated gamer. More than 70 percent of gamers play with a friend, and millions of people worldwide participate in massive virtual worlds through video games such as "Farmville" and "World of Warcraft," the article noted. Multiplayer games become virtual social communities, where decisions need to be made quickly about whom to trust or reject and how to lead a group, the authors said. People who play video games, even if they are violent, that encourage cooperation are more likely to be helpful to others while gaming than those who play the same games competitively, a 2011 study found.

So, to the dismay of many in my generation, limited and controlled video game play, and especially involvement in multi-player, first-person shooter games, can be good.

Video games can also help build a great deal of hand-eye coordination, which, coincidentally, is an essential skill to be a good shooter.

That very first game that was introduced, the Atari 2600, had a joystick with a single button on it. It also had a paddle, which was a dial to be used with the tennis and pong games. They were, by today's standards, very simple.

Today's newest game systems and the games they play on them require a great deal more skill and coordination. The average video game controller has eight to 10 different buttons and two separate joysticks manipulated with fingers. Pushing buttons and moving the separate joysticks in coordinated orders and motions have an effect on the play of the game. It is actually rather fascinating.

Video games today are played in three dimensions, with the ability to look around in a first person perspective. The relationship to shooting is simple… good hand eye coordination equals a better shooter. A better "natural" shooter makes for a positive initial experience.

FIREARMS IN VIDEO GAMES

Another benefit of video games is that many of them contain firearms as part of the game. These firearms are usually based upon actual firearms in use over time.

For example, in a World War II military game, the weaponry includes the M1 Garand, the Colt 1911 .45 ACP and even the Mosin Nagant Japanese bolt-action rifle.

One of the most popular games on the market today, "Call of Duty," includes numerous weapons with which the avid participants become highly familiar, including the Remington Model 700 .308 (the most popular sniper rifle in the world); the Beretta M9; various AR-15 platforms; the venerable AK-47 and many, many more…

These games are what are referred to as first-person shooter games. The entire game is played from the perspective of a person walking through the gaming area, in complete three-dimensional realism. So, how is this good?

Each weapon requires the player to aim in order to fire. There are different sight pictures for each different type of weapon. This includes telescopic sights with crosshairs, ghost ring-type sights, holographic sights, shotgun bead-style sights, and the common front post/rear groove sight.

I find that when I am introducing firearms to children who have played these games, they already have a basic knowledge of things like sight picture and how to aim and shoot. That, combined with the increased hand eye coordination abilities, can make for a positive overall experience.

Finally, when interacting with these avid gamers, I find that a lot of them know the exact type of weapon we are shooting or using for demonstration.

Many of them even know brand names that are commonly associated with the type of weapon we are using. For example, I was introducing some children to shooting an AR-15, and one of them asked me if it was an "ArmaLite," and did I have an Eotech holographic sight to try?

These children also experience a strong desire to try shooting.

NOW, FOR THE NEGATIVES

I believe that there are several glaring negatives to video games when it comes to their effect on youth and introducing them to firearms.

First, and foremost, the cardinal rule of firearm safety is that you never, ever point a gun at anything you do not want to kill or destroy. These games all go entirely against that rule, and make children comfortable with taking a sight picture on a human being. I'm not a big fan of that.

Second, because of the familiarity that a lot of these kids have with some of the weapons in the game, it can make them overly confident in their ability to use and operate safely what is a dangerous and complicated device. Also not a good thing.

Have you ever thought about the massive amount of influence these games can have on a young child?

For example, this is what Wikipedia has to say about the most popular first-person shooter game, "Call of Duty": "Call of Duty (commonly shortened to CoD) is a first-person and third-person shooter video game franchise. The series began on the PC, and later expanded to consoles and handhelds. Several spin-off games have also been released. The earlier games in the series are set primarily in World War II, including Call of Duty, Call of Duty 2, and Call of Duty 3. Beginning with Call of Duty 4: Modern Warfare, which is set in modern times, the series has shifted focus away from World War II. Modern Warfare

Overconfidence is not a good trait when learning firearms safety. Start with simple firearms and then move up to guns more complicated in components and actions.

EFFECTS OF FIRST-PERSON SHOOTER GAMES

On April 20, 1999, at approximately 11:19 a.m., Eric Harris and Dylan Klebold, both dressed in black trench coats, entered the school grounds and began shooting fellow students outside Columbine High School. They then moved inside the high school and began targeting random students and faculty. When it was all over, there were 12 students and a teacher dead, over twenty wounded, and both the community and the entire nation reacted in shock.

When the tragedy in Columbine, Colorado, occurred, the two youth involved were said to have learned how to use and become enamored by firearms from playing hours and hours of violent, first-person shooter games. I can't help but wonder, would things have been different if they were taught respect and safe handling of firearms?

(released November 2007) was followed by Call of Duty: World at War; and Call of Duty: Modern Warfare 2 Black Ops (released November 2010) takes place in the Cold War, while Modern Warfare 3 (released November 2011) takes place in a near-future setting. Black Ops II (released November 2012) takes place in the year 2025. Call of Duty: Ghosts was released in November 2013. In May 2014, Advanced Warfare was announced.

"As of November 11, 2011, the Call of Duty series had sold over 100 million copies. (emphasis mine) As of March 31, 2012, there are 40 million monthly active players across all of the Call of Duty titles, with 10 million users of the online service Call of Duty: Elite and two million paying annual members. Over 1.6 billion hours of online gameplay have been logged on Modern Warfare 3 since its 2011 release. Sales of all Call of Duty games topped US$10 billion, according to Activision." (emphasis mine) Source: http://en.wikipedia.org/wiki/Call_of_Duty

40+ million kids play that game, cooperatively every month.

Finally, I find that children who are heavy users and players of video games tend to spend the vast majority of their free time in front of a television set playing games and being hyperstimulated for, sometimes, hours on end. This tends to give them a short attention span (something that makes teaching a bit more difficult – just ask any grammar school teacher) and much more focused on indoor, sedentary activities than outdoor, active activities. I don't think this is a good thing.

Whether or not your child owns video games, and where and how often they play, is up to you as a parent. There are clear benefits to moderate use, but it seems evident that there is a detriment to children from the heavy use of video games.

CHAPTER SEVEN

Teaching the 10 Commandments

©National Shooting Sports Foundation, Inc.

The "Four Cardinal Rules of Firearm Safety" are:

    1. Always treat every firearm as if it were loaded.

    2. Always keep the muzzle pointed in a safe direction.

3. Keep your finger off of the trigger until you are ready to shoot.

4. Be certain of your target and what is beyond.

The following additional rules are part of a larger list, altogether known as the 10 Commandments, whose values vary slightly, depending on whom you ask or whose instructor program you ascribe to. They are:

5. Always keep your gun unloaded until ready to use.

6. Know how to use and operate your firearm safely.

7. Always wear proper eye and ear protection whenever you will be shooting.

GROWING UP WITH GUNS

The following is an excerpt from "Growing Up with Guns," by Steve Sorensen, copyright 2013, page 35. Used by permission. See if you recognize references pertinent to some of the commandments in it.

The Wrong Hands for Guns
I've never been shot, but maybe I've been lucky.

A close call came when I was a teenager. A buddy and I were walking up the trail alongside Hemlock Run. He tripped, and as he lurched forward to catch his balance he jammed the barrel of his .22 rifle into the soft spot just under my earlobe.

Call me lucky—if there's such a thing as luck. I was lucky his finger wasn't on the trigger. If his finger was on the trigger, I was lucky he didn't pull it as he instinctively tightened his grip. If he did pull it, I was lucky the safety was on.

Years later I met a local surgeon in the woods who looked at my shotgun and said, "Guns scare me. I've seen what they can do." I've also seen what guns can do, and they scare me, too. Guns by themselves don't scare me, but guns in the wrong hands do.

Careless hands are the wrong hands for guns. Careless hands are hands attached to an unthinking mind. On the day my friend jammed the barrel of his gun into my ear, he was carrying the gun in a cross-body position. Had he (or I) been thinking, he would have been pointing the gun the opposite way. The thinking gunner considers whether he should carry cross-body, or on the shoulder, or pointed down and forward, or up and away in front.

The hands of a person influenced by alcohol are the wrong hands for guns. Excess alcohol impairs judgment, and handicaps one's ability to assess his impairment. When I see beer in a camp it bothers me, but not because I oppose alcohol. It bothers me in the same way beer cans on the floor of a car bother me. Just as alcohol should have nothing to do with driving, it should have nothing to do with carrying and using guns. Alcohol can weaponize a person.

The hands of bullies and show-offs are the wrong hands for guns. Some people are victims of their own machismo, thinking they are as invulnerable as Muhammad Ali. There's a story about him refusing to buckle his seatbelt and telling a flight attendant, "Superman don't need no seat belt." She calmly whispered, "Superman don't need no airplane either." All men sometimes need to be reminded, especially when around firearms, that we're not Superman.

The hands of an angry person are the wrong hands for guns. A chip on your shoulder is best left home when hunting or target shooting. A fight with the wife or the boss isn't a good prelude to hunting. Anger can cloud judgment.

The hands of a poacher are the wrong hands for guns. There is a good reason for poachers and felons to lose their gun rights. Lawbreakers can be motivated to attack a person who might reveal their lawlessness.

The hands of a person who doesn't respect others are the wrong hands for guns. The inability to consider the rights of others, the lack of common courtesy, and the notion that anyone who is in the woods is in my way all reveal attitudes that invite trouble.

The hands of a person who doesn't respect guns are the wrong hands for guns. People must be taught respect for guns, especially in a day when young people see hundreds of murders on television and in the movies and are desensitized to the seriousness of firearms.

That's a good reason for gun safety to be mandated as part of our school curriculum. But now I'm dreaming.

Come to think of it, guns don't scare me as much as hands scare me. It is the hands that are unpredictable. In the proper hands, a firearm is a tool that can bring challenge and enjoyment to you. In the wrong hands, it can bring suffering and tragedy to many. So, whenever you pick up a gun, ask yourself, "What kind of hands are mine?" That's not a dream. It should be a reality for all of us.

8. Never use alcohol, prescription, or non-prescription drugs before or while shooting.

9. Use only the correct and proper ammunition for your firearm.

10. Never rely on a gun's safety as anything but a backup to your safe handling.

Each of these 10 commandments is ESSENTIAL to ensure your and your pupil's safety while using and being in the presence of firearms, both on the range and off. Let's evaluate the commandments one by one.

COMMANDMENT I

ALWAYS TREAT EVERY FIREARM AS IF IT WERE LOADED.

I extend this rule during instruction to "until you have personally checked it yourself, and then STILL treat it as a loaded firearm."

Before we begin, read through the following news reports and see if you can detect a pattern.

BLACKMAN TWP., MI — Police said a 16-year-old boy accidentally shot and killed his brother, thinking a handgun was unloaded when he pointed it at the 21-year-old.

The younger brother told authorities he took the handgun into his brother's room, and said something to the effect of, "Do you feel lucky?" before pulling the trigger, Blackman-Leoni Department of Public Safety Deputy Director Jon

Johnston said in an email.

Police have not released any names.

Johnston said the parents were at the grocery store and the brothers were the only people at the residence on the 5000 block of Big Rock Street in Stonegate Farms.

The 21-year-old was pronounced dead at the scene close to 7:30 p.m. Saturday, Dec. 6.

"This is clearly a tragic situation for the family," Johnston said. "We'll complete an in-depth investigation and determine what actions are appropriate from there."

(http://www.mlive.com/news/jackson/index.ssf/2014/12/blackman_township_accidental_s.html)

MASON COUNTY, Wash. -- The Skokomish tribe near Shelton is mourning the death of 14-year-old Ciqala Miller. Deputies believe he was accidentally shot to death by his 13-year-old friend as both boys pointed hunting rifles at each other believing they weren't loaded. In court documents, the boy said he and Ciqala had spent the day fishing and were playing around at Ciqala's house on Skokomish tribal land north of Shelton Tuesday evening.

"They were even arguing over who caught the bigger fish and playing and they both grabbed rifles and were playing and one of the rifles went off," said Mason county chief criminal deputy Ryan Spurling.

The 13-year-old immediately went looking for help.

"The young boy come running out and was asking us to call 911 and was really panicky," said neighbor Annette Smith. Smith said she was first at the house to find Ciqala on the floor of the hallway taking his last breaths with little chance of saving him.

"There was no way," she said.

Ciqala is from a prominent Skokomish family. His uncle is the tribal chairman. His father, Rick, is a prominent hunter. No word yet on whether the prosecutor will pursue the fact that hunting rifles were so easily accessible. "There are different firearms rules as far as has a child had a hunter-safety class, have they hunted, that type of thing. Handguns are different than long guns in some of those respects," Spurling said.

Smith is also a member of the tribal council.

"There are also accidents that do happen and this one here was a really bad accident," she said. "I really feel bad for both families."

(http://www.komonews.com/news/local/Friends-thought-rifles-were-unloaded-in-deadly-accident-264673951.html)

PACIFIC BEACH, Calif. - Police said a Navy SEAL is on life support after accidentally shooting himself in the head with what he thought was an unloaded gun.

CBS Affiliate KFMB reports that the unnamed 22-year-old was gravely wounded early Thursday at his Pacific Beach home while trying to convince a female companion that the pistol he was showing off was safe to handle.

The shooting left the sailor on life support at Scripps Memorial Hospital La Jolla, according to San Diego police. Authorities initially reported that the man had died.

. The serviceman, who had been drinking with a woman at a bar before they returned to his residence, was showing her his 9mm handgun when the accident occurred, San Diego Police Officer Frank Cali told KFMB.

The man (who mistakenly believed the gun was unloaded) offered to let his friend hold the weapon, according to Cali. When she declined, he tried to demonstrate how safe it was by putting it to his head and pulling the trigger.

The sailor, whose name was not released, had recently graduated from the Navy's Sea, Air and Land Teams program, which trains elite special-operations tactical units.

(http://www.cbsnews.com/news/navy-seal-shoots-self-with-gun-believed-unloaded/)

The national news is full of thousands of incidents where someone is injured or even killed by what is thought to be an unloaded firearm. The key point here is "thought."

You see, it is impossible for an unloaded gun to shoot someone or something. Every firearm has to have its projectile at least loaded in order for it to fire. Yet these accidents continue to occur. Too often, people are too confident in what they or somebody else has done, said or "thought" regarding a firearm. It takes a couple of seconds to check a firearm, and a firearm that is pointed in a safe direction while checking it will only hurt the ground, a tree, a wall or floor, which leads nicely into…

ALWAYS KEEP YOUR MUZZLE
POINTED IN A SAFE DIRECTION.

If you meant for them to happen, they would never be called accidents.

I'm sure that the people in the stories previously shared would change both their actions and the outcome in 100% of the situations, had they known what would happen.

Things happen. People forget things. People slip and fall. Mechanical safeties fail. Ammunition can be faulty.

These and a myriad of other things can cause a firearm to discharge at the least desirable times. If every time your gun goes off you have it with absolute certainty pointed in a safe direction, you will never have a situation that you may regret for the rest of your life.

The most important thing to remember with this commandment is that "safe direction" varies depending on your situation. People move unexpectedly. Pets and children do inexplicable things sometimes.

If you are on the main level of your home and your child's bedroom is upstairs, pointing your muzzle straight up is not a safe direction. That same rifle, when taken outside, can be pointed up in the air and be considered safe. Conversely, pointing the muzzle of your firearm at the ground can be the only safe option at times, but not if you are standing on a rock!

Always, always, always be aware of your muzzle and what it is pointed at. When introducing a youth to firearms, there is no such thing as too many times to remind them, "keep your muzzle safe" or "make sure you pay attention to where your muzzle is pointing."

Finally, never be afraid to quickly and forcefully take immediate control of a firearm and the situation.

A forceful "STOP!" and a redirecting of an unsafe action is always better than an accident.

KEEP YOUR FINGER OFF OF THE TRIGGER UNTIL YOU ARE READY TO SHOOT.

Firearms are designed to operate via a rather complicated mechanism called a trigger. The trigger is where man and muscle meet mechanics in a single point of control.

Remember our definition of "accident." Especially when instructing use in firearm use and safety, a moment of mental lapse can mean a serious consequence. Because a firearm is designed to fire when you pull the trigger, keeping your finger off of it will prevent an accidental discharge.

BE CERTAIN OF YOUR TARGET AND WHAT LIES BEYOND IT.

According to a Wisconsin hunting incident report from 2012, one of the most common causes of firearm accidents in the field is when somebody shoots and does not know what is beyond their target.

Lead shot fired from a shotgun easily travels several hundred yards and retains enough energy to embed in skin or damage an eye. A .22-caliber rifle bullet can travel well over a mile. Once you start firing larger caliber rifles, such as a .243 or a .30–06, that distance can extend to several miles.

Remember, once a bullet is fired it can never be taken back. Always know where your bullet might be, or might go, and err on the side of caution.

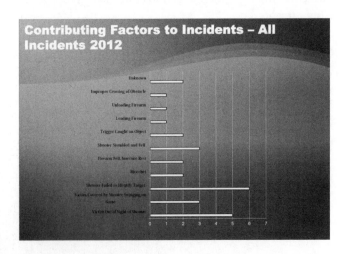

COMMANDMENT V

ALWAYS KEEP YOUR GUN UNLOADED UNTIL READY TO USE.

As the examples showed, many accidents occur with an "unloaded" gun that isn't really unloaded.

It takes only several seconds to load your gun for use, so there is no reason to have your gun loaded before you are ready to fire it. At the range, we always have firearms that are not actively being shot placed safely on their side or, if available, in a gun rack designed to hold them safely with actions open and, if neither option is practical AND safe, unloaded in a case.

COMMANDMENT VI

KNOW HOW TO USE AND OPERATE YOUR FIREARM SAFELY.

Firearms differ in their type (rifle, shotgun, or handgun); make (brand such as Winchester, Remington, or Browning); model and action type (single-shot, revolver, semi-automatic, bolt-action, etc.). Whenever you change firearms while introducing them to youth, you should revisit all of the areas and mechanisms of that particular firearm. Why is this important?

Imagine the following scenario. You have been working with a particular pupil for several sessions at the range with a bolt-action, single-shot .22 rifle. The safety on this rifle is located at the rear of the trigger guard. They have shown great enthusiasm and desire to fire a different type of gun. The rifle you hand them next is a bolt-action .223 that has a telescopic sight, and the safety is located on the rear of the action and is also a three-position safety.

Your pupil picks up the weapon, is rather excited, begins to go through the motions of checking it and searches for the safety. They immediately, when they realize that it is not where they expect it to be, turn the gun over and look at the trigger guard. In the meantime, they turn to you looking for instruction and at the same time sweep the barrel in an arc…

You can see where trouble can occur.

Every time you switch firearms, review the rules of safety, review the anatomy of that particular gun, and make certain they understand before you ever let them shoot it.

Thanks to advances in technology, you can now protect your hearing while hunting and not sacrifice your ability to hear what is happening around you, like you would if using foam ear plugs. The cost of these products has come down substantially.

Always wear the proper eye and ear protection when shooting.

ALWAYS WEAR PROPER EYE AND EAR PROTECTION.

You only get two eyes and two ears in your lifetime. Protecting them is essential.

Like today's computers and cell phones, the cost of quality equipment continues to drop as technology advances. Foam ear plugs cost about $0.50. You can buy a pair of electronic earplugs or shooting muffs that allow you to hear regular conversation yet block out loud noises such as gunfire instantaneously for between $30 and $40. If you wear prescription glasses, you will not need additional eye protection, but a high-quality, protective lens that meets ANSI Specifications can be had for under $10.

Are your eyes and ears (as well as those of your student/child) worth $50? I would happily pay 100 times that amount to regain the hearing I have lost from years in duck blinds and pheasant fields before electronic hearing protection.

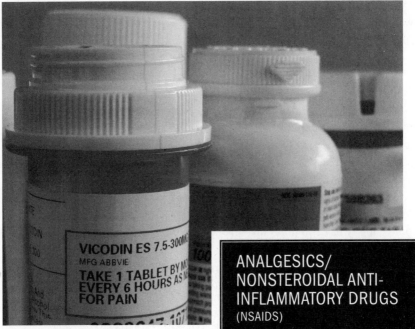

VICODIN ES 7.5-300M
MFG ABBVIE
TAKE 1 TABLET BY M
EVERY 6 HOURS AS N
FOR PAIN

Prescription and non-prescription medications can interfere with your ability to function properly, something that is not acceptable when handling a firearm.

NEVER USE ALCOHOL, PRESCRIPTION, OR NON-PRESCRIPTION DRUGS BEFORE OR WHILE SHOOTING.

I am so adamant about this rule that I have been known to step off of the firing line at a trap club if I have seen someone consume an alcoholic beverage prior to shooting. I have heard many different excuses along these lines.

"I only had one (or a few) beer(s)."

"Relax... I can handle it. I've been

ANALGESICS/ NONSTEROIDAL ANTI- INFLAMMATORY DRUGS (NSAIDS)

Even common pain-relieving medications can have unintended and unexpected reactions in certain people. Yes, you are unlikely to fall over from taking a Tylenol, but, again, stranger things have happened.

Common Analgesics:

The three most commonly used analgesics are Tylenol (Acetamino-phen) , Advil (Ibuprofen), Aleve (Naproxen Sodium) and Aspirin.

In addition, the following NSAID analgesics are commonly prescribed for chronic pain.

Celecoxib	Celebrex
Rofecoxib	Vioxx
Valdecoxib	Bextra
Parecoxib	Dynastat
Etoricoxib	Arcoxia

Combining any of these medications with alcohol can exaggerate and compound the effects. Drugs, alcohol, and gunpowder DON'T MIX!

shooting for a long time, even longer than I've been drinking."

"Don't be such a worrier."

That's the one that really gets me. I worry, even if it's just a little, every time I have a firearm in my hand, am near someone with a firearm, or even in the presence of a firearm standing against the wall, in a rack or on a table.

If I can't see that the action is open and the chamber clear from where I am, I will walk over, safely pick up the firearm, check it, check it again, and then put it down safely and only pointed in a safe direction.

Shooting a gun is a very serious responsibility that, if a momentary lapse of judgment has been made, can have serious and even deadly consequences.

Save the celebratory drinks for long after your guns have been cleaned and put away in storage.

The students and teenagers that I have taught get this rule repeated to them over and over throughout their instruction. Alcohol, drugs, and gunpowder don't mix!

COMMANDMENT IX

USE ONLY THE CORRECT AND PROPER AMMUNITION FOR YOUR FIREARM.

Remember, a firearm is a precision a piece of machinery. I use analogies with younger kids, depending on their age, to explain the different types of ammunition and different firearms. "You can't play an Xbox game on a PlayStation 3, right? This is even more important than that, because this can cause a serious accident."

They get it right away.

COMMANDMENT X

NEVER RELY ON A GUN'S SAFETY AS ANYTHING BUT A BACKUP TO YOUR SAFE HANDLING.

Safeties are mechanical devices used to prevent the trigger from being pulled. Mechanical devices can and do fail, and often at the worst possible times.

I consider the safety of a firearm to be the "backup to the backup." You are already treating the gun as if it was loaded and you already are ensuring it is pointed in a safe direction. It is as simple as that.

Fortunately, by adhering to the rest of the 10 Commandments of safety, the safety is a welcome backup.

CHAPTER EIGHT

Homework

©National Shooting Sports Foundation, Inc.

Homework? Isn't this all about fun?

Homework is to learning what nitrous oxide is to an automobile. When used properly, it can greatly add to speed and power. Conversely, when not implemented correctly, it can result in serious damage to the machine.

Regardless of whom you are teaching or introducing to firearms (and especially if they have never had any experience before) you will want to assign a bit of homework for them to work on and practice in between your informational/educational sessions.

Certainly with younger children, you will want to have the parents on board and involved. If they are your children, that makes it all the easier.

If a firearm belongs to the person that you are instructing, they can use their own firearm for practice. If not, I find that there are several, very good substitutes for an actual gun.

REPLICA FIREARMS

If you are serious about instructing more than a few people in firearm safety, usage and technique, you should invest in several, quality firearm reproductions.

There are many sources for these, and my advice is to search online and order from a reputable company that shows good positive feedback in their reviews.

These replicas come in a variety of colors and configurations, in the shape of shotguns, handguns and rifles. If you plan on shooting any type of tactical or AR-style platform, you should pick up one of those as well

If you are handy, as one instructor friend that I know, you can even use wood to make some replica firearms that approximate the size, shape and weight of the guns that you are using.

HOUSEHOLD OBJECTS DOING DOUBLE DUTY

If you don't want to spend the money on an arsenal of replica firearms, there are several household objects that can do double duty for your student to practice with when they go home.

Even a 2X4 board cut to the approximate length of the gun the youth is using will work. If you have the time and materials, color one end brown (stock) and one end black (muzzle).

A standard broom makes an adequate substitute for a long gun. For a handgun, I have had people go home and use everything from a small cordless drill to a hot glue gun to a creatively constructed set of Legos. The most important thing is that every "firearm" has a clearly defined handle and a muzzle end.

TOYS

Yes, toy guns can be used to practice some of the drills that we are going to go through as well. Anything that is a toy that approximates the size and shape of a firearm will work.

PRACTICE DRILLS

Now that you have something to practice with, what shall we practice?

Aside from failing to check a gun to see if it is loaded, the number two cause of firearm accidents is the improper or the unsafe handling of a firearm. This can include not maintaining proper muzzle control, such as turning around with the gun pointed out rather than up or down, not using the firearm safety or proper trigger control by keeping your finger off the trigger until you are ready to shoot, not being familiar with a firearm, not using the proper technique to walk with or cross obstacles with a firearm, etc.

Remember, at the beginning of every session with anyone you are introducing to a firearm, it is an essential practice to review and refresh the four cardinal rules of firearm safety:

Treat every gun as if it were loaded, keep your finger off the trigger until you are ready to shoot, always keep the muzzle pointed in a safe direction, and know your target and what lies beyond it.

Those four rules will prevent a great deal of issues related to firearm safety. There are more things that you as an instructor can and should do, however.

For young children, we modify these drills and also add the "Eddie Eagle" program teaching of "What to do if you see a gun" from Chapter 3.

The following homework drills, by no means all-inclusive, should help you and your pupils be safe, and avoid taking up "shooting time" at the range to train these skills.

Before we begin any drill, it is important to always remember that you should never, never, ever use an actual firearm that has not been double and triple checked to ensure it is unloaded and safe to perform any of these drills.

Drill #1: Pick up, check, walk, put down

This drill is exactly as the name indicates. The person picks up the gun/replica/object, checks it (or at least talks through and imitates the motions of checking it), uses a proper carry technique to walk across the room, maintains control of the muzzle, and puts it down safely.

Repeat three times, then add a partner who is instructed to do things at random for the final three to four times. The partner should walk around the gun side of the person holding the weapon, should randomly stop, should randomly walk faster, and do anything that may be unexpected to the person holding the firearm.

Advanced technique: Make the walk a bit longer and add different obstacles requiring the person holding the firearm to have to walk around, stop over, duck or otherwise maneuver in a way that makes it challenging to control the firearm.

Drill #2: Safe/unsafe

With a partner, the partner takes the firearm and holds, carries or places the firearm in various positions and then asks the students, "safe or unsafe?"

If the person you are introducing to firearms is going to be doing this drill with somebody else, it's best to give them some sort of informational sheet that explains different things for them to do.

Proper muzzle control is a critical aspect of firearm safety. (A: unsafe B: safer; C: safer D: unsafe)

Drill #3: Mount – Aim – Bang

I find this drill to be exceptionally useful when introducing someone to the shotgun, but it is useful with every type of firearm.

The youth, after ensuring the firearm is unloaded and safe, picks a spot and/ or target, identifies it, mounts the gun, takes aim and simply says "bang."

This drill accomplishes two things very well… It increases the speed at which the pupil identifies targets, increases the speed at which they mount the gun and obtain the target in the sights, and, when done properly, greatly increases their ability to have and maintain proper form.

Mount.jpg AND Aim-Bang.jpg: Mount – Aim – BANG!

Safety is the number one thing to consider whenever guns are involved. There is no such thing as "too safe."

Everyone you introduce to firearms should be quizzed often and at random on the four cardinal rules of gun safety until they can rattle them off without thinking about them and in any order.

BENEFITS OF HOMEWORK

By Gail Luciano, Educator for 30 years

There are many opinions for and against the value of a child doing any kind of homework. Many children will balk at the first use of the word. Some parents will argue that their child has too much homework, not enough homework, or they don't find it necessary for their child to have any homework at all.

Why, then, do educators continually require any type of homework from their students?

The main reason is to reinforce what the children learned at school while maximizing the time available for teaching. But, do children really learn from spending at-home time doing homework instead of participating in fun or extra-curricular activities which they enjoy a great deal more?

First, let's discuss how kids learn from doing homework.

This concept has been debated since education in schools began, but mostly it is from a combination of the active recollection of the previously taught concepts, the repeating of information to commit it to memory (such as in studying for a spelling test), and the physical act of writing and practicing the concepts that the student has learned.

Is homework necessary? There are actually numerous reasons for assigning homework.

Students might merely need reinforcement, or a review of new concepts they have learned while the content is still fresh in their minds and easier to recall. Sometimes students may need to finish an assignment they fell behind on due to lack of time or focus. Other times, homework is a longer or more involved assignment, such as a report or a project that cannot be finished during the normal school day or the instruction time available.

Homework can also simply be time allotted for studying for quizzes or tests. Many times it is just an added incentive that you try to help a student get more motivated in a particular area of study. So, outside of learning material content, what else do children learn from doing homework?

Assigning homework will, first, help a child develop responsibility for himself/ herself and his/her actions. He/she was given a task, now he/she must complete it and return it at the appropriate time. The child is held accountable. He/she needs to act independently of the teacher/instructor and make decisions on his/her own. Second, doing homework can help a child develop needed life skills like overcoming obstacles (I don't "get" this, so, how do I proceed, what should I do next, what do I need to do to figure this out?); communicating effectively (Will the teacher/instructor understand what I am trying to say or accomplish?); making decisions (What are the consequences if I do not finish this task?) and setting goals and achieving them (I am going to finish this task. Now it is completed.). These life skills, along with many others, are what help us accomplish our goals and live our lives to our full potential.

Finally, doing homework can help children learn to manage tasks efficiently. They have to be prepared to move through the task from its delegation to the finished product. They must plan, create, organize and prioritize. This involves a great deal of decision making, like, "What are my options?" and "What is important to me?"

Whether or not you assign homework to your charges is your personal decision as an educator/instructor. The decision should be based on your experience, expectations and what the individual child is capable of producing without unneeded stress.

Learning should be fun, be it instructional time or homework time. You, as the educator/instructor, should put every effort into making the experience interesting, meaningful, and perhaps most importantly, challenging enough to stimulate their learning, but easy enough to make it doable.

This requires a great deal of time and effort, as your job is to give every child the means to work up to his/her full potential. Therefore, you might have to be extremely creative, as each child has his/her own individual learning style.

Homework, if assigned for the proper reasons, can be extremely valuable to a learner, especially to one who may be struggling with a specific concept or task. Just because you are teaching to a large group doesn't mean you have to delegate a homework assignment to the entire group. Think about the individual student's needs and go from there.

Careful and specific assignment of homework can have exponential results. It will allow your students to understand core concepts while allowing you to maximize your time together without having to tediously repeat things.

For the best results, homework should be interesting to the student, meaningful, doable without a great deal of stress, and fun! Remember, the secret to quality teaching is to make learning an enjoyable experience.

CHAPTER NINE

Choosing the Right Gear

©National Shooting Sports Foundation, Inc.

This chapter could be an entire book in and of itself. Even as recently as 20 years ago, there were hardly more than a few different pieces of equipment suitable for younger children to use when learning about firearms, firearm safety and firearm handling. Most of that gear was full-sized shotguns and rifles sporting a shortened stock for smaller-stature people. Fortunately, there have always been .22 rifles, .410 shotguns, and patient adults to teach their safe use.

This recommended equipment list is by no means 100% complete. There are, certainly, other products by other manufacturers that may well suit your needs.

As we have discussed in previous chapters, you can teach firearms and firearm safety with a minimal amount of equipment – basically some sort of firearm, a safe and open space, something to shoot at and some ammunition.

We will start with the most essential piece of equipment... the gun. This list includes my recommendations based on over 20 years of instructing and teaching youth firearm safety, handling and use.

When you are shopping for a firearm for you (or one to use to teach and instruct other s to use) it can be rather overwhelming, as there are dozens of models that will suit the purpose. There are two things to remember that can make this process a great deal easier.

The first is that there are many youth size models of almost all of the popular firearms out there from every manufacturer.

People always ask me what the "best gun" is, either for themselves or for their child. While there are certainly models and manufactures that I prefer, there are very few bad guns out there today. We have been manufacturing firearms for so long (Beretta can trace their lineage back all the way to the 1500s) that the process, parts, fit and machining have all become rather standardized.

The second is in regards to price and quality. Yes, you can buy some rather inexpensive firearms. This is one of those times when you absolutely do not want to make a purchase simply based on the price of the product. Ask yourself this very simple question: Is the future of enjoyment of shooting/hunting/competing side-by-side with my child for their entire lives worth an extra $100, $200 or even $300?

When you decide to introduce your child to firearms, you should begin putting some money aside just for that purpose and just for them. Not only will it allow you more flexibility when it comes to buying equipment and ancillary gear for them, it will also allow you to spend more quality and enjoyable time with your child because, let's face it, everybody likes to get nice things!

It has reached the point in our house where I just have to casually men-

The first thing that I always do when checking the fit of a firearm to a youth is have them pick up the firearm and hold it in a natural and comfortable shooting position.

tion that I will be heading to our local big box outdoor store and my children clamber over one another to come along. Sometimes a major purchase is made. Sometimes they just get a candy bar or other treat. The point is they are animated and excited to spend time with me doing things that I also like to do. The same can be true for you.

The good news here is that firearms, unless abused, rarely lose their value. It has been my experience that youth firearms tend to hold their value even better than standard size firearms, because there are fewer of them in circulation.

You can feel confident that, when you purchase a firearm that fits your child and will allow them an enjoyable experience, when the time comes you will be able to trade up and purchase another, newer weapon for them that will offer the same benefit. If you start your children young, you may have to go through this process several times.

If you are introducing and/or teaching your own child the basics of firearm use and safety, it will be a bit easier for you than if you are planning to teach a number of other children.

In asking other long time gun people what they do when introducing youths to firearms, one rule of thumb has remained consistent when picking a firearm, and that is the "fit–feel–function" rule.

FIT

I have been shooting guns my entire life. I have probably shot different makes and models that number in the thousands. Most firearms are built to what that particular company considers average. That is, they build the drop at comb (the amounts that the area where your cheek meets the stock is below the sight plane of the barrel); the length of pull (the length from the buttplate to the trigger); and even the length of the forend (the forward end of the gun where the hand that is not on the trigger goes to support it) and balance point of the firearm to fit a certain-stature individual that they believe will cover the broadest range. As you can imagine, that leaves a great deal of room for interpretation.

I am fortunate to have acquired numerous shotguns and rifles over my shooting career, but there are several to which I specifically gravitate because they just "feel right."

This can also be translated to other sports and sports equipment. A baseball player uses a bat that has the proper length, balance, taper and dimensions to maximize their swing efficiency and power so that they can be a more consistent hitter. A golfer will perform best with clubs that are fit exactly to him or her. A club that is too long or too short poses a significant handicap when trying to play the game. A gun is the same way.

While not as important for the first few introductory sessions, if your child has desire to continue shooting, it will grow more and more important. This is doubly so if they decide to compete in any type of shooting events.

The first thing that I always do when checking the fit of a firearm to a youth is have them pick up the firearm and hold it in a natural and comfortable shooting position. There are several things you should look for right away.

Do they appear comfortable or uncomfortable holding the gun up? Does the gun seem too "front heavy?" Is their forward hand and arm at an awkward or uncomfortable angle or position in order to keep the gun held steady?

Does their shooting dominant eye line up correctly with the sights/bead of the gun?

How does the stock fit to their shoulder? Does it seem like they have their cheek farther back than it should be? Do they stand at an awkward angle (this is most often leaning backwards in order to compensate for a gun that is too long and/or too heavy)?

What type of firearm is it? If it is a shotgun, does it have a large, highly visible bead on the end that the child will have an easy time seeing? If a rifle,

Leaning backwards often occurs when the gun is too long and/or too heavy.

does it use open sights or telescopic sights? Telescopic sights (scopes) are some of the easiest sighting tools to use when instructing children, however, they are also rather advanced and I believe should be reserved for future sessions, with the exception being the youngest of children. In those instances, the enjoyment of the experience is the biggest key and making things easier on them will also make it easier on you.

If iron sights are used, what type are they? The easiest ones are the simple "post and V" that we are all familiar with. I will often actually take out a piece of paper and draw the proper sight picture to make sure that the child can easily acquire it while we are there fitting them for the gun.

FEEL

For the majority of my youth, I played baseball. I had a glove that became my preferred glove to use, so much so that I paid more to have it repaired than it would have cost in order to buy a new one. I could also pick up any bat and swing it a few times and immediately know whether I was interested in trying it out on the field or not. This is something that is much more based on the child rather than your observations, but you still need to be observant. You should also ask the child numerous questions regarding the feel of the gun.

How does it feel? Does it feel heavy? Can you hold it up okay? Are you comfortable? Is it easy to obtain a proper sight picture?

Have the child take a stance and pretend like they are shooting. See how long they can comfortably hold a proper stance before becoming fatigued.

Be aware that children tend to enjoy pleasing adults, especially when they think what they do will have benefit for them. Therefore, sometimes a child will give you the answer they think you want to hear. Observe them carefully when asking these questions to determine whether or not that is the case.

Remember, it is always better to find out something is not right and/or not comfortable at the store or when selecting from a number of different firearms than when you are already out on the range.

FUNCTION

This is the point where you will need to make a choice as to what type of gun you will buy.

If it is a shotgun, will it be a single-shot? Will you choose an over-and-under or a side-by-side? Perhaps a semi-automatic? What gauge will it be?

For a rifle, are you buying a gun simply for fun, or will it also be used for competition or hunting? A first firearm is rarely a deer rifle, but on occasion it is.

For a recreational firearm, will you choose a .22 or a .17 HMR? Will it be a bolt-action, a break-action, or a semi-automatic?

A handgun? Will you choose a revolver or a semi-automatic? What caliber?

Again, entire books have been written on each of these subjects. This being a book on the introduction of youth to firearms, I would recommend the following: If your child is young or you are taking them for their very first experiences with guns, I highly recommend you do so with somebody who already has the equipment or will let you borrow it. The last thing you want would be to spend hundreds of dollars on firearms and gear only to have your child not have any interest in shooting.

You may be like me and just want a reason to go buy another gun. For those who are certain their child is interested, or who have this in common with me, read on for recommendations.

SHOTGUNS

As mentioned previously, I am not a big fan of the .410 for a child's first shotgun. The .410 is a "shooters gun" that yes, produces minimal recoil, but also has minimal shot string and has many less pellets than even a light 20-gauge load.

I am also not a fan of most single-shot shotguns on the market today. Most of them have an exposed hammer (something that, in my experience, makes them less safe) and are extremely lightweight compared to their double-barreled, semi-automatic, or pump-action brethren. The only plus side to these firearms is that they tend to be rather inexpensive. If your child is big enough and you find the right recoil pad, there will not be issues with extended shooting sessions.

I, and the majority of the firearm instructors that I know, are fans of a youth-sized 20-gauge semi-automatic shotgun for a child's first shotgun or shotgun shooting experience. The reason for this is that a semi-automatic uses a por-tion of the propellant and gases from the fired round to cycle the action, and this process can significantly reduce recoil. Couple that with today's high tech, recoil-reducing pads mounted on the butt-stock of most firearms and you have a winning combination of pain-free experience with enough power to do the job.

Second-place goes to a pump-action 20-gauge with a recoil-absorbing pad mounted on it.

Following are my recommendations for youth shotguns:

Best value: Tristar G2 Youth 20-gauge Combo

This firearm is manufactured in Turkey (as are many of the firearms that we see on the market today, including Stoeger, CZ USA and others that are "branded") and is also marketed under two well-known names in the firearms world: by Mossberg as the SA-20 and by Weatherby as the SA-08 20-gauge. They are manufactured in the same factory to the same specifications for all three companies, but I prefer the Tristar for several reasons.

I didn't initially know why I was drawn to this gun until I had experience with it with several different youth of varying size…

The number one advantage to Tristar's package is that, in addi-tion to three stainless steel choke tubes, a barrel extender, and wrench in its own plastic case, it comes with a full set of shims as well as a complete second stock.

Remember our fit-feel-function rule? If you have chil-dren of your own, you most likely know how quickly they

can change sizes. We have had to buy new wardrobes for my teenage sons in as little as 90 days! That can be an expensive proposition when you are talking about a piece of equipment that can cost from several hundred to several thousand dollars. These accessories allow the gun to grow with the child.

As we also discussed, a semi-auto has the benefit of its action taking up some of the recoil generated upon firing. Any time that you can make shooting a more pleasurable experience, it is more likely to become a passion rather than an occasional pastime.

The best part is that this complete kit is priced at or less than most other semi-automatic shotguns on the market today. Unfortunately, the G2 Youth is only available in a right-handed model. Left-handed version is only available in 12-gauge models.

Mid range: Remington Model 870 Express Youth

The Remington Model 870 has been sold in greater numbers than any other sporting firearm, ever. That speaks volumes. Priced a bit less than the G2 combo, this "bullet-proof" shotgun is a great choice if you are on a tighter budget, and especially if you have multiple children who will be using it as they grow up and through their firearms use.

A re-vamp of the old-style, hard rubber recoil pads, the new Remington G3 soft pad keeps recoil manageable for all but the most sensitive shooters. Left-handed version is only available in 12-gauge models.

High end: Benelli M2 Field Compact

Benelli has been at the forefront of innovation in shotguns since the 1990s. The heart of every Benelli shotgun is the Inertia Drive system, a unique system that has only three moving parts, requires zero adjustments and is the ultimate in reliability. This style of action also allows for a much lighter and well-balanced shotgun. Combine that with the company's ComforTech recoil system that reduces felt recoil by over 48% and you have a gun that not only functions and feels good in hand, but is pleasant to shoot.

Available in both 20-gauge and 12-gauge, with left-handed version in 12-gauge only.

Benelli's Inertia Drive system has only three moving parts, requires zero adjustments and is the ultimate in reliability.

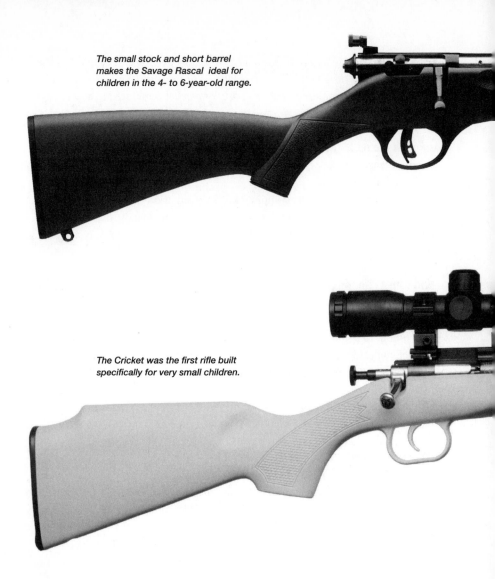

The small stock and short barrel makes the Savage Rascal ideal for children in the 4- to 6-year-old range.

The Cricket was the first rifle built specifically for very small children.

RIFLES

For a first rifle or rifle experience, it's hard to beat the venerable .22 long rifle. When introducing a youth to a rifle, I prefer a bolt-action simply because of its simplicity and safety, ease of loading and firing a single round at a time; the similarity to many of today's hunting rifles (the majority of which are still bolt-action); plus the benefit that a .22-caliber produces zero recoil regardless of the configuration. It's a win – win – win.

Following are my recommendations for youth .22 rifles:

Young children: Tie between the Savage Rascal and Cricket Youth .22

The Savage Rascal is created for young, small-stature shooters, is single-shot only and has some very nice upgrades for the price: Savage's Accu-Trigger system, one of the finest on the market, and an adjustable peep sight, rather than just a simple notch-and-post style.

These firearms, while very small, are still fully-functioning .22-caliber rifles and are certainly NOT TOYS.

Their small stocks and short barrels make them ideal for children in the 4- to 6-year-old range.

The Cricket is a pint-sized powerhouse built so much with kids in mind that the synthetic stocks even say "My First Rifle" on them.

The Cricket was the first rifle built specifically for very small children and has a unique safety feature that requires the user (or, more likely, the adult supervisor) to pull the metal disk at the back of the rifle in order to cock the firing pin. This means that even if a bullet is chambered, the gun will not fire until this step is performed.

.22 rifle best value: Marlin Model 925

This clip-loading .22 rifle represents one of the best buys around in a bolt-action repeater. It features a clean-lined, hardwood stock with swivel studs for an optional sling (a bonus if it will be doing double duty as a hunting rifle), a 22-inch Micro-Groove® barrel and a 7-shot clip magazine. I prefer magazine-style .22s to tube-fed.22s for the simple fact that they are easier to quickly load/unload and are much easier to check to determine if they are safe.

.22 rifle mid range: Ruger American Rimfire .22

Like the Tristar, American firearms company Sturm, Ruger & Company has build a platform designed to grow with a new shooter. Each Ruger American Rimfire® rifle includes two interchangeable stock modules that provide comb height options for scope or iron sight use. Standard models come with long

length-of-pull modules, while compact models come with short length-of-pull modules. By simply removing the rear sling swivel stud, stock modules can be changed in seconds. All four stock modules are completely interchangeable across all models. They also feature an adjustable trigger dubbed "the Marksman" that allows adjustment between three and five pounds of pull. The only reason that this rifle is not the "best buy" is the inexpensive price tag of the Marlin model 925.

.22 rifle high end: Ruger 77/22

Rare it is that the same manufacturer has two of the three recommended categories, but since the demise of Weatherby's Mark XXII, the Ruger 77/22 is

The Ruger 77/22 is the rimfire on the market that is built most like a typical, big-game rifle.

The Ruger American Rimfire® rifle
includes two interchangeable stock
modules that provide comb height options.

the rimfire on the market that is built most like a typical, big-game rifle, with
dimensions similar to their Mark 77 big game rifles, all the way down to the
larger bolt handle and "three-position" safety. With an SRP of $899 (and well
worth that price if you are serious about shooting), you can buy two or three
"standard" .22s, even from their own line.

AIR RIFLES

Second to the .22 rifles listed above (and if you are limited in your ability
to find open spaces to shoot), would be a high quality air rifle in .22 or .177
caliber.

These quality (and quite powerful) weapons can be fired in the backyard or
even the basement (be sure to check your local regulations first) with minimal
space, and can even be used to hunt small game later on. In addition, you can
pick up pellet ammunition for a very reasonable price – usually under $10 for
500 shots, and even cheaper with some less premium brands.

I recommend pellet rifles for two reasons. Lead pellets ricochet less than

steel BBs, and airguns made to take
only soft-metal pellets tend to be much
more accurate than those that shoot
BBs or combination BB/pellet rifles.

Gamo "Little Cat"

The Little Cat is the newest addition to the Youth Precision Airguns family from Gamo. With a 36-inch overall length and 525 fps with Match Lead Pellets, the Little Cat Airgun has been designed specifically for young shooters. It incorporates a wood stock, metal barrel, and comes standard with fiber optics sights. There is also a grooved cylinder for optional scope/optics mounting. The Little Cat Airgun is great beginning firearm to involve young shooters in shooting sports while teaching them the basics of shooting safety and target competition.

Stoeger X3

This is a gun that won't disappoint. At just over four pounds, and with a relatively easy cocking mechanism, even young children should be able to comfortably handle and shoot it. One of the best warranties out there and a suggested retail price of $100 means it doesn't break the bank, either.

HANDGUNS

This is certainly not the most common scenario, but does occur, therefore, we should address both the concept of children and handguns, the conflict of many

state, local, and national laws, and some of the reasoning behind why a handgun might not be the best choice for an Introduction to firearms.

I will never forget the first hunter safety course I took when I was nine years old. There were numerous, actual and fully functional firearms in the room with us. There was a representative of each type of firearm, as well as several different actions of each type. For shotguns there was a bolt-action, a pump-action, a semi-automatic, and an over-and-under. For rifles, there was a bolt--action, a single-shot, break-action, a semi-automatic and pump-action. For handguns, there was a toy revolver, a replica 1911 toy pistol and, finally, there were a couple of the paper roll cap–style cowboy six gun replica toys.

One of the first questions asked was, "Why do you have real rifles and shot-guns, but only toys for the handguns?"

Instead of answering, the instructor called one of the adults to the front of the room. After picking up one of the shotguns and checking it to see it was unloaded, he handed it to him and instructed him to hold it out from his body at an angle. He said to the entire class that it was never, ever okay to ever point a gun at anybody for any reason and then walked around him while instructing the man to swing the shotgun and try and point it at him. As you can imagine, it was a bit of a comedy of errors with them circling and turning one way and then the other and finally twisting around turning the gun upside down and looking over his shoulder in order to point the shotgun in the man's direction.

The instructor then did the same thing with one of the toy handguns. When instructed to turn and point the handgun at him, the man simply turned his wrist and the gun was immediately pointed at the instructor. "That's why," he stated. "Because even though we never, ever load these guns inside and even though we ALWAYS check each firearm multiple times before and in each class, it is easier to avoid an accident ever happening when you use something that can

At just over four pounds, even young children should be able to comfortably handle and shoot the X3.

only hurt me or you if we are hit over the head with it!"

That demonstration made a powerful impact even to my young mind. Firearms are dangerous and potentially deadly tools. While the situation was somewhat lighthearted, it demonstrated the fact that it is much easier to control a long, long barreled firearm from the instructor's point of view than it is a small, short-barreled firearm.

I highly encourage that, even if you would like to introduce your child to a handgun and that is the weapon that you will be purchasing and shooting together, at least for your first few sessions you use a long gun of some type. Once the basics of operation, procedure, handling, and safety are gone over, you can then easily transition those skills to a handgun.

Plus, the government has its own views on youth and handguns.

The Gun Control Act of 1968, 18 U.S.C. Chapter 44, provides in part as follows:

18 U.S.C. 922(x)

The following is the "Notice" from the ATF rule:

YOUTH HANDGUN SAFETY ACT NOTICE

(1) The misuse of handguns is a leading contributor to juvenile violence and fatalities.

(2) Safely storing and securing firearms away from children will help prevent the unlawful possession of handguns by juveniles, stop accidents, and save lives.

(3) Federal law prohibits, except in certain limited circumstances, anyone under 18 years of age from knowingly possessing a handgun, or any person from selling, delivering, or otherwise transferring a handgun to a person under 18.

(4) A knowing violation of the prohibition against selling, delivering, or otherwise transferring a handgun to a person under the age of 18 is, under certain circumstances, punishable by up to 10 years in prison.

There are certain states that interpret this rule to mean that no child under the age of 18 shall "possess" a handgun – AT ALL.

ALWAYS CHECK YOUR STATE LAWS PRIOR TO ALLOWING CHILDREN UNDER THE AGE OF 18 TO HANDLE OR FIRE A HANDGUN.

If you do not own nor have access to any types of long guns, but have handguns (and, more specifically, have the specific type of handgun that the child will be shooting), I would still advocate that you start your first sessions with a toy such as a plastic dart gun or similar.

When choosing a handgun, the fit–feel–function rule will be magnified, as the vast majority of handguns are built to fit an "average" adult's hand. With every firearm, but especially in this case, improper fit is asking for an accident with potentially fatal consequences.

Many handguns in the larger calibers have smaller handgrips designed for women or smaller-framed male shooters. ©National Shooting Sports Foundation, Inc.

Young children should, when deemed ready, shoot nothing larger than a .22-caliber handgun and, after demonstrating safe knowledge, skill and handling of that firearm, move up to possibly a larger caliber such as a .380 or 9mm.

There are several, quality .22-caliber revolvers and smaller-framed semi-automatic handguns out there that will fit a youth well enough for them to shoot, and many firearms today in the larger calibers have smaller handgrips designed for women or smaller-framed male shooters that will suit your purpose.

WHY I HAVE A LOVE/HATE RELATIONSHIP WITH AIRSOFT

Even if you are not already aware of what an airsoft gun is, your child most likely is. Airsoft rifles shoot a small, plastic pellet of .24 caliber (6mm) at velocities between 400-500 fps from what are more and more realistic-looking and functioning replica firearms.

Airsoft rifles shoot a small, plastic pellet of .24 caliber (6mm).

Crosman 1911 pistol.

There are now airsoft rifles that mimic the most technologically advanced military assault weapons, ones that are identical copies to the colt 1911 and the Beretta model 92, as well as just about every other major firearm manufacturer's popular guns.

There are airsoft rifles manufactured to resemble hunting rifles, some complete with functioning optics. There are others that are replicas of shotguns that fire several pellets out at once to mimic the shot pattern experienced with a typical shotgun.

As you can imagine, there are many, many practical uses for these replica firearms to be used in the instruction and introduction of youth to firearms. I have used many of them myself, up to and including safe indoor shooting sessions with the youths I was instructing.

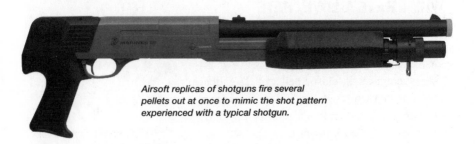

Airsoft replicas of shotguns fire several pellets out at once to mimic the shot pattern experienced with a typical shotgun.

Make no mistake, though, these "toys" are still very, very dangerous.

And that brings up the other side of the discussion. Marginalizing the danger to which you're exposed by replicating a firearm as a toy can build up and insensitivity to risk or, at the very least, allow habits to be built that can have deadly effects when transferred to their real counterparts.

Whenever we use an airsoft (and in the past 10 years I have yet to meet a child that I was using it with who did not know exactly what it was) we have the same type of safety instruction as we do when we use the "real" guns.

We talk about all the same dangers, all the same handling precautions, how to check it to see if it is loaded and, most importantly, we reiterate and reinforce the fact that we never ever, ever point this or any gun at anything we do not want to kill or destroy.

We use eye protection when shooting the airsoft guns, and at least talk about the fact that if we were using a firearm that shot bullets instead of plastic pellets, we would make sure we used ear protection as well.

I urge and encourage you, if you choose to purchase one of these airsoft weapons, that you maintain the same safe control, handling instructions and access to them that you would any other firearm.

There are now airsoft rifles that mimic the most technologically advanced military assault weapons.

OTHER RECOMMENDED GEAR: RECOIL-REDUCING ACCESSORIES

Throughout this book we talk about introducing youth to firearms with guns such as a .22-caliber rifle and/or air rifle. The main reason for this is recoil.

Dictionary.com defines recoil as "to spring or fly back, as in consequence of force of impact or the force of the discharge, as a firearm."

Put simply, recoil is the impact felt to the shoulder when shooting a rifle or shotgun as a result of the firing of that gun.

We've all heard the physics adage that for every action there is an equal and opposite reaction. Recoil is the reaction of the firearm to a shot being fired out the end of the barrel.

Improperly introducing someone to recoil can give that person a significant aversion to shooting guns. A great deal of the introductory process of shooting is done with specific steps taken to avoid a bad experience with recoil.

My very first shotgun was a Beretta Companion single-barrel 20-gauge. It weighed almost nothing, had no recoil pad and was way too long for me. It also had substantial recoil. I was already well into my shooting career at that point, though, and was hardly affected by those bad experiences.

We found a slip-on rubber recoil pad that, while slightly lengthening an already long gun, helped tame any recoil I experienced shooting on the range.

Back when I started shooting there really was no such thing as a youth gun. The only option was to take a standard manufactured shotgun and cut a couple of inches off the stock. The challenge here was, of course, that there were also not many recoil pads manufactured to a smaller butt end of stock dimension.

Fortunately for children who want to shoot, that is no longer the case. There are many, high-quality firearms that are both fit and balanced specifically for a small frame shooter. Thanks to technology, there are also some fantastic recoil reducing pads and inserts that can remove recoil from the experience almost entirely.

SHOCK EATER RECOIL TECHNOLOGY

The ShockEater® Recoil Pad is the latest advancement in energy absorption and recoil dispersion. Simply put, it keeps you shooting longer, while increasing accuracy, comfort and consistency with your long guns. Made with proprietary Nano-Poly™ technology, the ShockEater Recoil Pad is designed to reduce peak felt recoil without increasing length-of-pull or altering appearance. At only 8 mm thick and 1.4 ounces in weight, it provides superior shock absorption in a form that is lighter and thinner than any foam or gel can provide.

The ShockEater Recoil Pad is conformal to the shoulder area, supporting proper gun fit and improving pitch and toe angles at the butt-stock. This combination of unique fit and absorption properties allow for maximum comfort and reduced felt recoil. More comfort, less pain means hitting your target with greater consistency. The ShockEater Recoil Pad is compatible with many of the leading shooting vests and shirts, making it the optimal accessory for a variety of shooters from first-timers to seasoned veterans.

The ShockEater Recoil Pad is designed to reduce peak felt recoil without increasing length-of-pull or altering appearance.

So, what exactly is "Nano-Poly technology?"

What this means is that ShockEater works at a molecular level. When moved slowly the molecules within the polymer will just slide past each other, making the material soft to touch. But when a high-energy impact occurs (like a shotgun recoil) the molecules grip onto one another, locking together, to become almost solid for just a few milliseconds before releasing and becoming soft once again. It's during those few milliseconds that the molecules quickly absorb the recoil and transfer it into thermal energy. As the molecules in their near-solid state try to slide past each other, they create molecular friction – heat. This friction is spread throughout the molecules of the entire pad in just milliseconds – so fast it never heats up to the touch. It seems like the energy just disappears. That's also why they call it the ShockEater … it will literally "eat" the shock and vibration associated with recoil.

I have used this product with both youth and adults firing everything from 20-gauge shotguns to .375 H&H and .416 Rigby dangerous big-game rifles and everything in between. This amazing product works, and works well!

SHOCKEATER YOUTH COMBO PACK

This combination package includes everything that the new or youth shooter needs to begin safe, recoil-reduced shooting: Shockeater recoil pad; Shockeater

The ShockEater combination package includes everything that the new or youth shooter needs to begin safe, recoil-reduced shooting.

Youth orange shooting vest, designed to be used with the Shockeater Recoil Technology pad; a set of reusable earplugs and a set of ANSI-rated eye protective glasses. All at a price that is significantly less than the purchase of all of the items separately.

SHOCK POD RECOIL REDUCER

A slip-on product to fit most any gun, the Shock Pod recoil pad from Recoil Tech opens up the range of possibilities for youth shooters. Children often start their shooting experience with a .22 rifle and move up as they get older. Major factors in determining when a young person can move up to a larger rifle or shotgun include the child's size, strength and pain tolerance.

The Shock Pod, from Recoil Technologies, comes with customized options for every shoulder shape. They are twice as wide as the gun stock, which reduces the pressure by half to the shooter.

Many young shooters want to shoot the more powerful guns but the recoil is too intense for them to shoot comfortably. The strong recoil of a big gun leaves bruises, creates flinching in anticipation of the recoil and affects shot placement. This can all lead to frustration and lack of desire to progress to harder recoiling guns or the continuation of shooting altogether. By reducing the amount of felt recoil, the experience becomes more enjoyable and successful.

With the recoil reduced, firearms become much more manageable for younger shooters. Young marksmen can see improvement much more quickly and easily as they build their skill without the worry of jolting recoil.

LIMBSAVER RECOIL PADS

Limbsaver pads are designed to specifically fit a wide variety of rifles, shotguns and muzzleloaders, so that you can use the same rifle/shotgun that you have without adding additional length of a slip-on pad. These recoil pads incorporate anti-muzzle jump technology and can reduce up to 70% of felt recoil. They are easily installed in seconds and are built for all-weather conditions.

Limbsaver has become such a successful product that some manufacturers license their technology to come standard on their firearms. They are also available in slip-on and custom, grind-to-fit models.

Limbsaver pads can reduce up to 70% of felt recoil.

CHAPTER TEN

The Demonstration of Power

MAKE SOMETHING HAPPEN

Use "reactive" targets. When introducing kids (or anybody) to shooting, forget boring paper targets. Ringing or knocking down steel targets is much more exciting and gratifying. Rocks, pieces of brick or cement blocks fly off when hit, often leaving a cloud of dust. Plastic water bottles filled with colored water are spectacular when hit with a high-velocity round like a .223 Remington. Red Kool-Aid is cheap and the results are instantly gratifying. You might even slip in a Tannerite target as a surprise. There is plenty of time later to learn how to shoot groups on paper, but to generate and keep their interest use targets that react.

– Bryce Towsley,
noted outdoor writer and author

Several times in this book you have heard me refer to the demonstration of power when first introducing youths to firearms at the range. A demonstration of power is a central part of the learning process of guns and shooting. This is not meant to be used as a scare tactic to put a fear of firearms and firearm safety into a child, but rather a learning experience to demonstrate the fact that, no matter how small, a firearm needs to be always treated with the utmost care and respect.

If you have spent some time shooting for fun at various targets, you may recognize some of the tactics that are explained in the coming instructions. If not, I urge you to go out and experience these reactions to a bullet hitting different targets for yourself before you set up this demonstration.

Ideally, I like to do this demonstration with three different calibers/sizes of projectile to demonstrate a point. If you do not have the option of three different calibers or sizes of projectile, simply proceed with the caliber at hand.

My preferred calibers for a demonstration of power are the .223 Remington, the .22 long rifle, and .177 caliber air rifle.

.223 REMINGTON

I choose the .223-caliber because it is a high-velocity projectile that, when loaded with a softpoint or hollowpoint bullet, results in violent reactions downrange on some relatively large targets such as gallon jugs of water, watermelons, cantaloupe or grapefruit. They will completely evaporate an orange.

In addition, the .223 Remington has a very traditional rifle cartridge shape, meaning it has a relatively large brass case compared to its bullet, with a defined neck and shoulder, and is fired with a separate primer from the case.

As Bryce Towsley commented in the beginning of this chapter, gallon jugs and two liter bottles filled with water and food coloring or a package of Kool-Aid make a spectacular display when hit with a .223 Remington, and especially if there is snow on the ground. No snow? I have also done this demo in the summertime using an old white sheet to give a blank background so that the pupils can see and experience the reaction.

Finally, all of these pluses to the .223 Remington are further enhanced by its ability to be fired by even the youngest of shooters with no noticeable recoil.

If I have a group of entirely new shooters, I will fire the rounds at my chosen targets. Should I have some experienced shooters with me or in a group, I let one of them fire at the downrange reactive target.

.22 RIMFIRE

The choice of this caliber is also twofold. While the .22-caliber rimfire has the same bullet diameter as the .223 Remington, the cartridge tends to be (or at least noticeably appears to be) smaller in size compared to the .223.

A .22-caliber rimfire produces zero recoil, a moderately loud "bang" upon fire, and has a differing mechanism of igniting the powder. Rather than hitting a primer that is inserted separately into the cartridge case, the .22-caliber rimfire has the primer loaded into the "rim" on the bottom of the cartridge. The primer strikes the rim near the outer edge, igniting the primer chemicals, which ignite the powder in the cartridge case.

The cartridge case is also noticeably different, as a .22-caliber rimfire case is completely straight with no "shoulder or "neck," as well as being significantly smaller than the cartridge case for the .223 Remington.

.177-CALIBER AIR RIFLE

The increased popularity of guns and shooting over the past decade or so has been a real boon to the air rifle market. Many people who have chosen to go out and buy their first firearm, be it traditional rifle, shotgun, handgun or modern sporting rifle, have found that, while they are a great deal of fun to shoot, they require significant space and, in the case of an urban or suburban resident, usually a long trek to someplace safe to shoot. That can cause frustration should someone wish to practice their shooting more often or in shorter duration periods closer to home.

The nice thing about an air rifle is that, with very minor expenditures of time and money, an air rifle can be fired in the backyard and even the basement. (Be sure to check and comply with local ordinances, and use an appropriate backstop. A cardboard box full of old telephone books and/or newspapers is often adequate to stop a pellet.)

Furthermore, an air rifle works via a pneumatic pump, a cartridge of compressed air or a spring piston to force air under pressure through the barrel when the trigger is pulled. This means that there is no cartridge, primer or powder, but rather simply the (usually lead) projectile. The pellet is also noticeably smaller than both the .22-caliber long rifle and the .223 Remington in both length and diameter.

Finally, the increase in the purchase of air rifles has increased competition in that space, leading to a much higher quality product at a lower available price point than ever before.

SETTING UP THE DEMONSTRATION

The very first thing I do is present the three different types of ammunition I will be using for the demonstration. I tell students which cartridge/projectile is which caliber, and which gun I will be using them in. Then, I asked them several questions.

What are some of the features of this cartridge? How does the .223 cartridge differ from the .22-caliber rimfire cartridge? Do you notice something different about the .177-caliber pellet? What is it?

Most children who have never seen these different types of cartridges will have questions and comments. One of the most frequent questions you will get is what makes the pellet fire, if there is no case, powder and primer? Remember, everything about introducing youth to guns is about safety and having fun. Having a great deal of engagement in the form of questions and answers is a great way to introduce knowledge, and more knowledge equals a greater degree of safety.

To be most effective, the demonstration should be set up at a relatively short distance so that your intended audience will have an "up close and personal" view of the reaction of the target.

I prefer to shoot three, different sized targets – one for each caliber.

For the .223 Remington, I most often use a gallon jug or two liter bottle filled with water or water that has been colored with Kool-Aid. That jug, at between 50 and 75 feet, when shot with a hollowpoint or frangible bullet from my bolt-action .223 Remington, creates a large burst and spray of liquid, as well as significant damage to the gallon jug or 2-liter bottle.

Moving on to the .22 rimfire, I most often use a soda can that has been filled with water. My bullet of choice (and also regardless of which bullet I have shown them in demonstration) for the .22 rimfire is a hyper-velocity, hollow-point bullet. When the bullet strikes the can of water, it also produces a very large splash and significant damage to the can, most often creating a large jagged hole and even sometimes blowing the can into two separate parts.

For the .177-caliber air rifle, I usually choose an unopened can of soda. This choice is simply because this usually creates a more "visual" reaction immediately upon the pellet striking the can than if it were filled with plain water. A flattop pellet or one of today's new "hi shock" pellets enhances the visual impact of this demonstration.

After the initial "shock and awe" of the violently reacting targets, I send the students to retrieve all of the pieces.

Next, we discuss what happens to each target and why. I discuss how bullets work, the concept of mushrooming as well as hydrostatic shock, but only to the extent that demonstrates a bullet can make a much larger hole than its diameter.

As some of the targets are too mangled to use for the next demonstration, I ask the students what things can they name that are approximately the same size as the targets that we have just shot?

There are all kinds of answers…

They sometimes talk about toys, other similar sized objects, etc.

Then, after holding up the damaged gallon jug, I take an empty, non-shot gallon jug and hold it up next to or in front of one of the children's heads. Then I move it down across their body to show them the approximate area a gallon jug will cover.

Next, I bring out a "trump card" to demonstrate why we are always cautious around firearms. "Who knows a lot about the human body?"

I then explain that the human body is made up of over 70%… WATER! While explaining this I again take the jug and hold it up to my head, to my chest, to my leg, across my arm, etc.

It always is a sobering moment for them.

Next, I hold up the .223 cartridge next to the .22 cartridge.

"Even this much smaller bullet and cartridge can do a tremendous amount of damage if it manages to hit somebody's body."

I hold a can up to my face and ask, which side do you think I could do better without? They often laugh, but then I explain, "imagine the damage from this can right here, or here (moving it down to the middle of my chest) or here (moving it out across my arm)."

Finally, there is the portion that I call "the speech."

"Remember… What we have here is something that can be a great deal of fun, and something that you hopefully will enjoy doing for the rest of your life. It is also a very dangerous and deadly weapon when mishandled or used improperly.

"This dangerous weapon can hurt you, it can hurt me, it can hurt your parents, your brothers, your sisters, and other people that you love and care about. It can hurt your dog or cat. It can hurt people standing next to you and it can hurt people standing far away from you.

"Because of this, we are always very careful and we always, always follow the 10 Commandments of gun safety whenever we are holding or near firearms. Safety is something that we take very seriously here, and if we feel there is an unsafe situation, we will immediately correct it.

"It is nothing against you and it is nothing against any person who makes a mistake. That's why we are here. To teach and prevent mistakes. Is everybody okay with that?"

I have found in both teaching and my decades long sales career that one of the most important portions of every interaction where you are trying to convey a point or message used is to gain agreement. Always ask for the child's agreement with every question that you ask or lesson that you are teaching.

Notice that the speech is rather short and very much to the point. Remember our two rules… Number one when we shoot we are always safe. Number two we have fun.

Keeping the lessons short but to the point enhances the "fun" portion of your teaching interactions.

In my surveys of the youth I have introduced to firearms, one of the things they report that most stands out is the demonstration of power. However, the largest impact I have found this demonstration makes is on the student's parents when they talk about what happened, or perhaps they get to even see directly. They are amazed at how deeply engaged the children are and the impact that it seems to make on their conscience.

Kids are smart…and that is good news for you!

CHAPTER ELEVEN

Putting Deadly Power in a Child's Hands

©National Shooting Sports Foundation, Inc.

In Chapter 2, we discussed how old is "old enough" for introducing a child to firearms. The short answer is that there is no such thing as too young to teach firearm safety, and the level of introduction depends on the child.

If the child you're introducing to firearms is your child, you will have extensive knowledge about the level of maturity, the compliance with rules at home, the way they interact with other children, siblings, and adults, and, perhaps most importantly, how they may react to what I refer to as "responsible" situations.

We perform the demonstration of power to give a visual representation as to both the enjoyment that can be experienced when using firearms as well as the results and possible consequences that occur after the trigger on a firearm is pulled. A question I am often asked is, when is a child responsible enough to put that power in their hands?

Always remember – once fired, a bullet can never be "un-fired" or "called back."

The answer is a bit complex. I am fortunate that in over two decades of working with children and firearms, many of whom had no firearm experience other than seeing them on television, I have never been involved in any firearm accident.

It is my belief that this is because each child I instruct is thoroughly evaluated as to their level of knowledge, openness to instruction, interaction with others and behavior prior to putting a gun in their hands. It is that evaluation that helps determine when and if a child is responsible enough to shoot safely.

Here are some steps that you can take to determine when and with what level of responsibility a child is ready to shoot a firearm.

LEVEL OF KNOWLEDGE AND ITS IMPACT ON READINESS

A child's level of knowledge of firearms will change over the course of your interaction with them. If a child has never seen, handled or shot a firearm and is not familiar with the rules of gun safety, the introduction to the physical act of shooting a firearm will be different than someone who has already gone through an introductory safety program, such as the NRA Eddie Eagle firearm safety program.

As the level of knowledge, comfort and responsibility changes, you can change your method and means as to how they are allowed to shoot. For example, if you are starting a very young child in firing an air rifle, you may sit the child in your lap, rest the air rifle on a solid rest, place the firearm in proper position so that they can obtain the proper sight picture, help them hold the air rifle steady, and then coach them through the process of firing their first shot.

At the other end of the spectrum, you may be instructing a preteen or teenager in firearm safety and shooting. If they have demonstrated an understanding of the concept of the safety instructions and have a level of familiarity with the weapon already, you may allow that youngster to practice the proper safety check, load the firearm, get into a comfortable shooting position, obtain a sight picture and to fire their first "live shot" all on their own.

OPENNESS TO INSTRUCTION

There is only one person in charge when introducing youths to firearms... you.

Whether in a one-on-one situation or a small group, your each and every command must be met with absolute obedience. A child who shows a great deal

The method and level of control you maintain while a child is holding and firing a firearm will depend on the child and include their size, knowledge level and ability.

Many times you will find it easier to control and maintain safety by using terrain or other objects. Here, the author has a first-time shooter firing at clay targets from inside a wooden "box." The box helps to limit the range of motion available to swing the barrel.

of resistance to your instruction will demand more "one on one" attention than one who hangs on your every word of instruction and agreeably follows your commands.

INTERACTION WITH OTHERS

A child's habits and behaviors when interacting with others should be carefully observed and used to evaluate the method and means of how you will allow them (or even if you will allow them) to handle and shoot a firearm.

If instruction is to take place in a one-on-one situation, you may want to thoroughly interview their parents and get answers to some of the following questions: Does the child demonstrate leadership tendencies, or are they more of a follower? Do they listen well to instruction, or are they rebellious and try to disrupt what you are doing when others are around? Have you determined their motive for being with you? Is it to spend quality time with you? To experience something new? To "do what mom or dad does"?

If it is a child that you will be mentoring that is not your own, is that child engaged and actively participating in the activities? Are they there because they want to be there, or because mom and dad made them come?

If in a group situation, do you feel that a certain child would perform better and/or be more safe in a one-on-one situation?

BEHAVIOR

It is been my experience that children who are being taught the safe and proper handling and use of firearms respond best to an immediate and continuing reminder of who is "in charge" while they are there. I have no reservations about removing a child from group instruction, or calling a complete stop to instruction for the day with a child in a one-on-one situation.

When it comes to firearms, safety is not optional. Safety is mandatory. Any type of risky or disruptive behavior that would interfere with anyone else's ability to participate, learn or perhaps endanger their safety is immediately addressed, and usually rather firmly.

It sometimes takes several outings or observations to geet everything to the point where you will be in effective synchronization with the child and your lesson and instruction will be seen as enjoyable while also remaining safe.

When in doubt, always err on the side of safety.

Here is some good news…

In all of the years I have been interacting with youth and guns, I have not met a child who was unable to be instructed in safety and participate in safe shooting, even if that meant some special and additional accommodations needed to be made.

In addition, there are many studies on child behavior and child psychology that demonstrate a unified opinion on children and responsibility: The more responsibility and the younger the child who is given the responsibility, the more responsible they tend to be at all of their childhood stages.

CHAPTER TWELVE

The One Rule That is Never Violated

Throughout this book, we have referred many times to the safe handling of firearms. By following the 10 Commandments and, more specifically, the four cardinal rules of gun safety, there should never, ever be any accidents with a firearm. That seems a bold statement, but it is absolutely true. Let's briefly revisit:

The Four Cardinal Rules of gun safety are:
- Always treat every gun as if it were loaded.
- Always keep the muzzle pointed in a safe direction.
- Keep your finger off of the trigger until you are ready to shoot.
- Be certain of your target and what lies beyond.

The rest of the Ten Commandments are:
- Always keep your gun unloaded until ready to use.
- Know how to use and operate your firearm safely.
- Always wear proper eye and ear protection whenever you will be shooting.
- NEVER use alcohol, prescription, or non-prescription drugs before or during shooting.
- Use only the correct and proper ammunition for your firearm.
- Never rely on a gun's safety as anything but a back up to your safe handling.

While every one of the 10 Commandments are important, there is one rule that, on its own, will prevent most every accident. Can you guess which one?

Here's a hint: This one firearm safety rule is also related to EVERY OTHER FIREARM COMMANDMENT when it comes to SAFETY.

If you guessed rule number two... you'd be close but you would have guessed wrong. (I'm a big fan of rule number two, because guns that are pointed in a safe direction don't kill people.)

It's RULE NUMBER ONE - but WHY?

There is a reason that this rule is first. A firearm, on its own, is not dangerous at all. You can place an unloaded firearm in the middle of a crowded room, and the only way anybody would ever become injured by it is if they trip and fall over it.

You can drop an unloaded firearm. You can take apart an unloaded firearm. You can safely transport an unloaded firearm by any means.

You see, a firearm is just like any other tool out there. It requires human intervention and interaction in order for it to function according to its designated (or undesignated) purpose. The problem occurs when we have not personally verified that a gun is unloaded and that the chamber and magazine are empty.

The following is a quote from my favorite book, Robert Ruark's "The Old

It is just as easy to form good habits as it is to form bad ones. ©National Shooting Sports Foundation, Inc.

Man and the Boy" (copyright 1957 Holt, Henry & Company):

"Habit is a wonderful thing," the Old Man said. "It's just as easy to form good ones as it is to make bad ones. Once they're made, they stick. There's no earthly use of slipping the safety off a gun until you're figuring to shoot it. There's plenty of time to slip it off while she's coming to your shoulder after the birds are up. Shooting a shotgun is all reflexes, anyhow.

"The way you shoot is simply this: You carry her across your body, point-ing away from the man you're shooting with. You look straight ahead. When the birds get up, you look at a bird. Then your reflexes work. The gun comes up under your eye, and while it's coming up your thumb slips the safety and your finger goes to the trigger, and when your eye's on the bird and your finger's on the trigger the gun just goes off and the bird drops. It is every bit as simple as that if you start at it right. Try it a few times and snap her dry at a pine cone."

I threw the gun up and snapped. The gun went off with a horrid roar and scared me so bad I dropped it on the ground.

"Uh huh," the Old Man said sarcastically. "I thought you might have enough savvy to check the breech and see if she was loaded before you dry-fired her. If you had, you'd have seen that I slipped the shell back when you weren't looking. You mighta shot me or one of the dogs, just taking things for granted."

That ended the first lesson. I'm a lot older now, of course, but I never forgot the Old Man taking the gun away and then palming that shell and slipping it back in the gun to teach me caution. All the words in the world wouldn't have equaled the object lesson he taught me just by those two or three things. And he said another thing as we went back to the house: "The older you get, the carefuller you'll be. When you're as old as I am, you'll be so scared of a firearm that every young man you know will call you a damned old maid. But damned old maids don't shoot the heads off their friends in duck blinds or fire blind into a bush where a deer walked in and then go pick up their best buddy with a hole in his chest."

There are actually a few of the 10 commandments in this passage and, if you read the book, you will realize that there are dozens of references to proper handling and care of firearms. (If you want an excellent book on "coming of age" that you can read with your child, this is an excellent collection of short stories, each that teaches a rather profound lesson.)

We would never point a loaded firearm at another person, and a friend, a pet, our parents, our neighbors, or any object that we cared about. (Rule two- always keep the muzzle pointed in a safe direction.)

I repeat this rule many, many times over the course of introducing a youth to firearms. I ask, "How do we treat every firearm?" And not move forward with our lesson until the question is appropriately answered.

You'll recall from the news clips in Chapter 7 that several of the incidents were caused by a gun believed to be unloaded. Following that one simple rule would have saved those lives.

Would you shoot your gun in your living room? Most likely not. If you pick up a firearm that has been standing in the corner, would you pick it up and pull the trigger? (Rule number three- keep your finger off the trigger until you are ready to shoot, and rule number four-be sure of your target and what is beyond.)

What if you are uncertain as to whether or not a gun is loaded? By treating EVERY gun as if it were, you will be safe until you personally verify that a gun is unloaded and safe. (Rule five- Always keep your gun unloaded until you're ready to shoot.)

Different firearms have differing mechanisms for their action, many completely unrelated to the others, such as the difference between a bolt-action and a single-shot rifle. How can you stay safe with an unfamiliar firearm? Treat it like it's loaded. (Know how to use and operate your firearm safely- Rule six.)

Always keep the muzzle pointed in a safe direction.

If you don't have your earplugs in, will you damage your hearing? Yes, you will if the gun goes off. Treat it like it's loaded and make sure it is safe until you put your plugs in and you won't have a problem. (Rule seven, always wear eye and ear protection.)

If you follow rule number one and rule number eight, you will treat a gun like it is loaded and not handle it if you've had alcohol or prescription drugs.

Treating a gun as if it's loaded keeps you and your companions safe while getting the proper ammunition (rule nine).

Every gun is loaded, it is always pointed in a safe direction.

I have ingrained this NUMBER ONE RULE so thoroughly in my own children that each time a firearm is picked up, it is pointed in a safe direction and the action cycled, chamber physically inspected, and magazine viewed to ensure it is unloaded.

Many times we will unload firearms, place them in their cases and then inside a vehicle, and move locations. We know with absolute certainty that each of those guns placed in those cases is unloaded and safe.

When we reach our next destination, we remove the guns from their cases, point them in a safe direction, cycle the action, physically inspect the chamber and magazine to verify that they are unloaded, and then proceed, safely, to our next shooting activity.

Why do we follow the same steps each and every time we pick up a firearm?

Because of rule number one. Always treat every firearm as if it were loaded. Every habit is created by repetition. Repetition of this process creates good habits, and good habits with guns are safe habits!

Like "The Old Man" said, "It's just as easy to form good ones as it is to make bad ones. Once they're made, they stick."

CHAPTER THIRTEEN

Your Child's Friends, Neighbors, Teachers and Relatives

C hildren are by nature curious and rather vocal. They enjoy pleasing other people (especially young children), and also like to impress their peers and those from whom they seek approval. This desire for approval and to please can be a great asset when introducing a child to firearms, as well as in later lessons on skills and safe shooting. It can be a detriment, however, when it comes to other people they come into contact with who may not be as "firearm friendly" as you.

Here are some helpful tips and guidelines in preventing problems or misunderstandings, as well as protecting your child when dealing with friends, neighbors and teachers.

TALKING WITH FRIENDS ABOUT FIREARMS

Have you ever given your child something special, perhaps something that was a little bit out of the ordinary? One of the first things they most likely wanted to do with that special item was show it off to their friends. If and when your child has his or her own firearm, you can expect the very same behavior.

Remember – children like to please and impress. The rules with a firearm, however, are a bit different.

For my oldest daughter's 10th birthday, she received her very own shotgun, as she was old enough to participate in the state's youth hunting seasons and showed both desire and skill in clay target shooting. Her birthday is in August, and one of her very first questions was, "Can we bring my new shotgun in one day for show and tell?"

"No, we cannot, but we can take a picture of you with your new shotgun and, if you like, we can talk to the teacher about letting you talk about it during show-and-tell time."

Unfortunately (and unbeknownst to her) the idea was shot down almost immediately by the teacher and backed by the principal for fear of "creating questions they weren't comfortable answering."

It is a shame that we live in a society today where we have to worry about everything that may come out of a child's mouth as being misunderstood, misconstrued or, in some cases, even twisted to follow an agenda. Though there are many people who are open to firearms but not specifically pro-firearms, and others who are pro-firearms, there are also others who are anti-firearms, and you can count on somebody being offended.

There is that old phrase that you can't please all of the people all of the time, and that is clearly the case when it comes to guns. Prepare yourself for this fact and understand that it is nothing against you or your child.

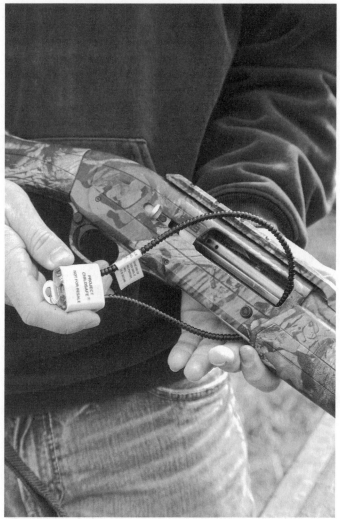

Take every opportunity to both practice and teach firearm safety. ©National Shooting Sports Foundation, Inc.

I was taught from a young age to not talk about the numbers or types of guns that we had in the house. I still believe that is a good idea, as there are nefarious persons in the world who may use that information with malicious intent. Usually, that means someone looking to steal a gun or a friend of a friend looking to steal a gun, or the assumption that because you have guns you also have a lot of money. (Alas, if that were only true.)

Yes, the incidence of these persons is probably rare of course, depending on the area in which you live, but they are out there.

While what you are comfortable sharing with others is entirely up to you, I advise you to take the path of caution, at least initially. Why risk it?

I also believe that children should not be exploited in order to affect the parent. What do I mean by this? There is been increasing concern regarding the questioning of children during their annual medical exams regarding whether or not there are guns in their home. That question is right up there with, "how much money do your parents make?" In other words – it is not really anyone's business whether or not I own something that is not only legal, but that is specifically addressed in the bill of rights of our Constitution. Anyone that walks into my home will immediately realize that there are firearms there, if for no reason other than there are many taxidermy mounts hung on the wall.

I have talked to my children and the children who I have mentored into firearm shooting and ownership that it is certainly okay to be excited and talk about your new gun. I am also careful to explain to them that they also need to realize that some people may not be pleased, nor will they be impressed with the fact that they have a firearm, and that's okay, too.

I have always allowed my children to show their friends their new firearm in the control of my home or a shooting range. I also use that opportunity as a chance to both practice and teach safety. I am often surprised at the reactions from children not familiar with guns, as well as the behavior of the child with the firearm in handling it safely.

I find that children also love to teach their peers, and will say things like, "you can hold it but first we have to check and make sure it is empty."

Finally, in teaching children about firearms, firearm handling and safety, and firearm ownership, I teach from a position that owning a firearm is no more extraordinary than owning a car or a house. Lots of people have them, some are nicer than others, and all should be respected.

PROPER STORAGE OF FIREARMS IN THE HOME

I am an advocate of gun safes and/or locking, steel cabinets to store firearms in a home. There are several reasons for this.

Firearms are dangerous when handled improperly, and the best way to prevent improper handling is to have absolute control over access.

It seems that even those who are uncomfortable with firearms to the extent that they may not allow their children to visit our home are often put more "at ease" when assured that our firearms are stored unloaded and locked in a safe to which only my spouse and I have access.

Do you leave your jewelry out on the kitchen counter? Firearms, in addition to having the potential to be dangerous, are also rather valuable. An easy way to prevent theft of anything is to lock it up.

Just say "NO" to a wooden gun cabinet with a glass front. While these types

Firearms, in addition to having the potential to be dangerous, are also rather valuable. An easy way to prevent theft of anything is to lock it up.

of storage cabinets can be attractive and show off your firearms collection, the same thing that makes them hat way also puts them at risk. Glass can easily be broken in a theft situation and the locks on these types of cabinets, if they even have them, usually are easy to overcome.

RECOMMENDATIONS: SAFES

Without a doubt, Cannon Safe has the best warranty in the safe business. Cannon Safe offers a zero cost lifetime replacement policy. The lifetime policy includes hassle-free 100% no-cost repair or replacement after a burglary, fire or natural flood emergency. They also manufacture many different sizes and models for every need and budget. They are also the parent company of GunVault, manufacturers of small, lockable containers for handguns that can be chained to a bedframe or bolted to a nightstand.

RECOMMENDATIONS: CABINETS

Homak Corporation has been manufacturing cabinets since 1947 and was at the absolute forefront of gun cabinet manufacturing since the early 1980s. Their cabinets feature a top and bottom lock, and come pre-drilled so you can bolt them to the floor or wall in your home, both an additional deterrent to theft.

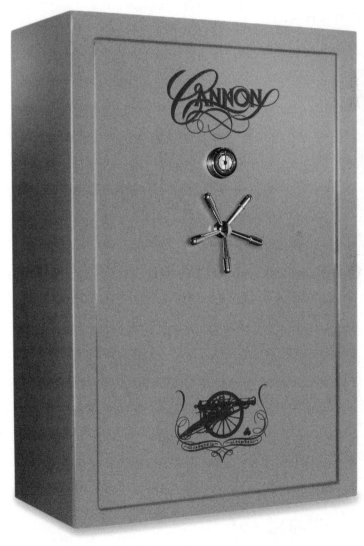

Cannon provides its customers with the best value in the business, an excellent product, at a fair price, with the best warranty available.

STORING HANDGUNS

Many people own handguns for personal protection and are wary of locking them up, as they feel it defeats the purpose of having the gun in the first place. After all, if you can't reach your principle means of self-defense in time, what good is it? The problem is that, as we previously discussed, children are curious. No matter how well you think you may have "hidden" your handgun, there is an excellent chance that your or someone else's child will find it.

GunVault Corporation has solved this problem. They manufacture an entire line of discreet, secure, lockable storage systems designed specifically for immediate access by an authorized person to a defense firearm. Using a combination of numerical combination, "finger combinations" and even biometric analysis, GunVault's products keep a firearm absolutely secure until you need it.

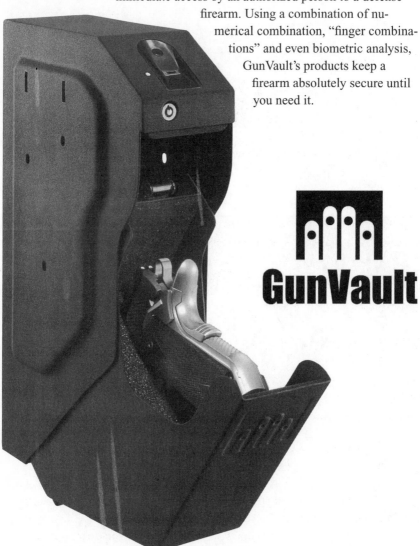

GunVault

HOW TO DEAL WITH A NEGATIVE EXPERIENCE

Guns and gun ownership can be a relatively polarizing topic. Your child's friends or parents may have a strong reaction and objection to your child shooting a firearm. There have even been instances where well-meaning parents misinterpret something a child has said and wind up making phone calls to child protective services, the police, the PTA, etc., thinking that they are "protecting" a child from some evil deed.

With today's increased awareness of the concealed and open carry of firearms, there is even a nefarious new term given by people who are anti-gun to the process of intentionally calling in police on a gun owner – it's called "swatting" (because a police SWAT team usually responds) and can have serious and even deadly consequences.

Hopefully the most you will have to worry about is someone saying something negative to your child about guns.

When this happens, it is important to take the child aside and speak to them about differences in opinion and how just like not everybody likes chocolate ice cream or broccoli, some people don't like or understand guns and shooting. Kids get it rather quickly.

I instruct children that if their friends or friends' parents say anything negative about guns they should just remain calm and tell them that they are always safe when they shoot and that in their house they believe in gun ownership, and that they should immediately tell me/their parents about what happened.

This conversation is also better had before a negative experience occurs. Remember, at many stages of a child's life, peer pressure is a motivating and molding factor in their social status and acceptance. Preparing a child to "diffuse and deflect" a polarizing topic can prevent consequences from a heated interaction between two children who, most likely, both know little about the facts, opinions and politics of guns.

TEACHERS AND SCHOOL

I am often amazed how people entrusted to educate our next generations of citizens can sometimes be so ignorant of both the law and peoples civil rights that they would speak of and even discourage the use and possession of guns. But it happens. It actually happens quite a bit.

There was a day when most schools, (even those in urban areas like Chicago and New York) had shooting as one of their physical education activities, some even having their own range and firearms on school grounds!

How sad we have come so far away from that model of teaching every child both the enjoyment that can be had from shooting guns as well as the serious danger that they can possess.

Unfortunately, due to the heinous acts committed by some seriously mentally ill people at schools with mass shootings, there is an extremely heightened sensitivity about children and guns. This heightened sensitivity extends even to the mere discussion of guns. Children have been thrown out of school for pointing their fingers at other children in pretend handgun fashion. They have been expelled for making a piece of bread in the shape of a gun.

It is absurd, I know, but the fact that it happens means that we need to address it and address it thoroughly before it is your child, or a child who you teach, who is in that situation.

DEALING WITH THE EDUCATION SYSTEM AND FIREARMS

Every year we have a parent teacher conference or open house at the beginning of the school year in order to meet and talk with the new teachers who will be responsible for our children for that school year. It is during this time that my wife and I have what we have dubbed "the conversation" with each of my children's teachers.

This conversation was brought about by an incident with my younger son and a school staff member misunderstanding something that he was talking about with shooting guns. He was rather young, and as young children do, they were talking about "good guys and bad guys." My son said that if he was dealing with a bad guy he would simply take a gun and shoot him. A fairly straightforward answer for a six-year-old child.

A portion of that discussion was overheard by a teacher, misconstrued and concluded with a referral to the principal's office and a visit with the school psychiatrist, as well as a very concerned phone call home.

I started off our "mandatory meeting" afterward incredulous that such a minor incident as speaking about shooting bad guys (and I don't know about you, but I recall that even the old-time westerns out there had "good guys" and "bad guys" who were always shooting at each other) could result in such a frenzied and detailed response. I often wonder if there would be the same reaction if my children spoke of pounding nails with a hammer, as many assaults and homicides are committed with them as well.

I begin these conferences discussing how we live in a violent world with people who intentionally cause harm and do bad things. I also talk about how we desire to keep communication lines open between the school and us regarding our children. Then I explain to them that in addition to it being a part of my business, my children both own and regularly shoot firearms.

To my children, having a gun is as common as owning a car or having a pet. They think nothing of it and are taught all of the safeties and responsibilities of safe firearm use and handling. They are talked to about and believe that a child having and shooting a gun is a completely normal process and think nothing of talking openly about how often and how well they shoot. My children, from a young age, have also each had their own pocketknife. They were taught similar safety measures and safe and responsible use of a knife. In our house, knives and guns are tools that are similar to hammers and drills. They have a purpose and are used for that purpose. They are never used for anything outside their intended purpose or that may put them or somebody around them in danger.

I ask them to, if they hear my children speaking of guns, reserve judgment on any conversation, and if they have any concerns to immediately contact me and I will speak with both them and the child.

As your child gets older, and because of the proliferation of organizations such as the scholastic clay target association, these conversations become easier to have and the teachers have seemed to be a little more open.

The most important thing regarding children, firearms and school is that conversations are had prior to them attending so that there are no misunderstandings by people with good (or bad) intentions.

DEALING WITH ANTI-GUN PARENTS

This can be a delicate situation. Unfortunately, we have known children who, once the parents became aware that we are a firearm-friendly home, do not allow their children to come over and play. It is a rare instance, but it does happen.

Remember, again, that your two goals when introducing children to firearms is for them to be safe, and to have fun. Not being able to play with their friends is no fun.

This is one of the few instances where I will not pursue a conversation with those parents, but rather simply allow my children to go over to their house to play and interact or to be involved in school and in after school activities with them. Children (especially young children) should not be put in the middle of a battle between parents, as they are still at a point that they do not understand differences in beliefs and values. Besides, I've found that most times these parents are not even open to the discussion.

A gun is a great responsibility, and with that responsibility is the requirement that you prepare your child to handle most situations they may find themselves in smoothly and, most importantly, safely!

CHAPTER FOURTEEN

Shooting Sports and Competition: Friend or Foe?

A fter initial introductions, safety instructions, lessons, and live fire sessions at the range, your student (child) may need some additional help in moving along in their firearms education.

It is here that we usually introduce competition. That competition can be as simple as keeping track of hits and misses and competing against themselves, to comparing scores in a group, to using active targets, like "shooting trees" that have students trying to swing a target from one side to the other by hitting it with a fired shot. There is a unique aspect to that game in particular, as part of the strategy can be to shoot your competitors targets back over from your side to theirs.

Some targets are more fun to shoot than others.

In all the years that I have introduced youth to firearms and firearm safety, I have never had a negative experience with competition that was introduced at the proper time and in the proper way.

If you watch your child in their progress and shooting skill, you will be able to easily determine when they are ready to experience some form of competition. They will become more and more excited when they hit a bull's-eye or knock over empty soda cans. If you were teaching a group, you will most likely see them start to compete with one another with comments such as, "I got two bull's-eyes… How many did you get?"

Many people have concerns about introducing young children to competition, but, as stated above, I have not seen anything but positive results. Tweens have already experienced competition and competitive sports for several years.

Also important to remember is that shooting and firearms are the "great equalizer," allowing students of small stature to easily out-perform shooters

NATIONAL 4-H SHOOTING SPORTS

The epitome of athletic achievement is the Olympiad. This sport is an Olympic event. Only two other sports attract more participating countries.

Generally speaking, if a young man or woman is not proficient in a sport by the time they enter high school, there is little or no chance that they will be permitted to participate in a school sport. Most coaches want established winners. This sport does not require previous experience. As a matter of fact, it is very possible for a person to start in this sport as a high school junior and compete on a national level before they enter college.

In some sports an athlete's peak performance will ebb at 16 years of age, other sports at 20, and still others at 28 or even 30 years of age, but beyond the age of 30, an athlete is definitely "over the hill." Not in this sport. This sport has had a national champion who was over 60 years old and also a 16-year-old, and every age in between.

There are girl's sports and boy's sports, but this sport is both.

There are indoor sports and outdoor sports. This sport is both.

There are winter sports and summer sports. This sport is both and is featured at winter and summer Olympics.

Football requires a team, while an individual can compete in track. This sport offers individual participation, team participation, or both at the same time.

Chances are, the high schools in your area do not offer one sport with a zero injury records. Serious injury is a part of most sports. This sport is the safest of all sports.

Sports arenas, courses, courts, gymnasiums and the like, use up a great deal of real estate and usually cost millions of dollars. This sport requires little more than a 50-foot long by 20-foot wide room.

This is among the most disciplined of all sports. Many students report a marked improvement in their ability to concentrate when they apply the principles of this sport to their academic pursuits.

"Purity" is a term used in sports to describe the degree of precision with which a physical function must be executed. This sport requires the highest degree of purity.

Sportsmanship: "quality and conduct of a person who accepts victory and defeat graciously." In many sports it is not unusual to see one athlete physically attack another. To date there is no record of such behavior in this sport.

In most sports, physically handicapped people are treated like invalids (which, by the way, they resent). Not in this sport.

College scholarships are awarded in this sport. These scholarships can be won by both men and women on the same team.

In most sports, qualifying for a team is not a guarantee that one will get a chance to play. Coaches enter their best athletes and the rest sit on the bench. In this sport, everyone participates.

(by: R.A. Soldivera. Reprinted from 4 H Shooting- http://w3.4-hshootingsports. org/Name_this_sport.php) of large stature. Completely opposite the outcome if they were in a wrestling match!

Competition offers the opportunity, for a child who may have had no success in competitive sports up to this point, to experience a win without devaluing it in any way. What do I mean by that? I mean that they come by that win honestly. The holes in the paper don't lie. The knocked over targets can't be cheated, nothing takes away from the value of their win, because they earned it. You will find that this matters to all children, but especially so with boys.

Starting in the pre-teen and continuing into the teenage years, boys are constantly in competition with one another. They compete for grades. They may compete in athletic contests. They compete for the attention of their peers. They compete for the attention of girls. Thus, introducing another form of competition to them is a natural progression, something they eventually expect in everything.

In his book, "Boys Adrift," Dr. Leonard Sax delves a great deal into the scientific literature and behavioral studies and also draws on more than twenty years of clinical experience as an MD PhD Psychiatrist to explain why many of today's boys and young men are failing in school and disengaged at home. He shows how social, cultural and biological factors have created an environment that is literally toxic to boys. He also presents several practical solutions, sharing strategies which educators have found effective in re-engaging these boys at school, as well as handy tips for parents about everything from homework to videogames to medication.

One of the main components of that re-engagement is competition.

John Tauer, professor of psychology at the University of St. Thomas, in St. Paul, Minn., studies competition and also is head coach of the men's basketball team. He says, "You don't get away from competition unless you go to a system where everybody gets to do what they want whenever they want."

"The combination of cooperation and competition result in greater satisfaction and often in higher scores as well. Kids prefer the combination of competition and cooperation. It's a significant increase in enjoyment. One of the biggest culprits in psychology is wanting kids to feel good all the time; trying to avoid competition is making it bigger than it needs to be."

In addition, and according to numerous studies about competition both in sports and in the classroom, the data is almost unanimous that competition increases focus, increases participation and, most importantly, increases both learning and results.

So, how can you introduce competition to your introductory program for your child and make sure it is done the right way? That is, in the way that the child responds to and improves?

The following are some tips and games that we have had great success with in both structured in non-structured programs.

SHOOTING FOR SCORE

This works very well if you are on a range that only allows you to shoot paper targets. (We recommend some initial shooting experiences outside of a structured range where you will have some more flexibility.)

For a standard, 50-foot, .22-caliber scored target, the bull's-eye is worth 10 with concentric rings moving outward from 9 to 1. Any hit outside of the scored rings scores a zero.

"Shooting for score" works well if you are at a range that only allows you to shoot paper targets.

The youth takes five shots at the target after which the hits are scored. High score wins. You can vary this game by having multiple children shoot from different positions, and even mix up those positions while they are all shooting. For example, shooter number one shoots from the prone position. Shooter number two shoots from the standing position. Shooter number three shoots from the sitting position. You can then have winners per round, winners per position and winners overall. An ancillary benefit to this is that there are multiple chances for each child to experience a win/success.

Variations on this game can be shooting reactive targets where, for example, knocking over one of the targets equals a score. Best out of five wins. You can introduce timing into this game as well, allowing shots to be taken only over a certain time period.

You should always keep a close watch over students in order to ensure that everybody is still engaged and, most importantly, that everyone is still having fun.

Remember – fun equals participation. Fun participation equals enjoyment and excitement and desire. Enjoyment, excitement and desire equals a lifelong love of shooting and shooting sports.

THE SINGLE-SHOT COMPETITION

Best used with a "scoreable" target system, this competition allows for only a single shot at the same target. You may define the shooting position or, as a

Sometimes the only competition that a young shooter needs is themselves. Shooting for and keeping track of score and progress often encourages them to perform better.

variation, allow the child to choose whatever position is most comfortable for them. The rule remains the same, though − one shot. The closest shot to the bull's-eye wins.

Many times in this competition your students will be at a more advanced level and shots will be very close and difficult to score. The simple solution to this is to increase the distance. If shooters are still keeping it so close that you have to have multiple shoot-offs or extended measuring times to determine a winner, increase the distance again.

A variation on this game is to use a shaken soda can at 100 yards (or further if necessary).

The way to make this game last longer and more fun is to not explain the theory of "walking" your shots into a target. They will eventually figure it out, and you may even have the shooters spotting for one another − calling their shots left, low, right, high, etc.

The first one to explode their can wins.

A windy day can make this game a great deal of fun.

ADVANCED GAME: THE SHOOTING TREE

I like these types of targets, as they introduce variety and challenge to the game.

A shooting tree has a number of targets vertically along a post. The targets swing from left to right or right to left depending on how they are set at the beginning of the game. The object of the game is to get all of your targets shot and hit so that they swing over to your opponents side.

This game introduces two variables, however, in that there is a time limit for the game, you can implement an ammunition (i.e., number of shots) limit to the game, and you can shoot targets that have been knocked to your side back over to your opponents side. As soon as all targets are on one side, a victor is declared. If time runs out, whoever has the least targets on their side is declared the winner.

A warning for this game… You now have two children shooting, loading and concentrating on several different things at the same time. It is very important to maintain focus and attention on both students so that no safety rules are violated. If you experience any type of malfunction or jam, the game is paused, guns are unloaded and cleared, and the game is begun again. You may have some complaints at first, but safe is always better than sorry. A brief explanation that takes into consideration the child's new love of competition and desire to win should alleviate any concerns.

Besides, the consequence of this is that they get to shoot more!

SHOTGUN COMPETITIONS

When shooting a .22-caliber rifle or air rifle, you will have the benefit of a stationary target and the child being confined to a shooting line. If you are introducing a youth first to the shotgun, or any of the common shotgun games, there are several things that you should take into consideration.

The first recommendation is to always let children first shoot a shotgun at a stationary target. The reason for this is twofold. First, it lets the child experience the mechanics and dynamics of the shotgun and recoil without having to also concentrate on moving the barrel with a moving target. It also will give them success and a completed sight picture, one of the key images you want their eyes and brain to comprehend... the "breaking" of the clay target.

After shooting several stationary targets, they should be ready in this or a successive shooting session to shoot at a flying target.

All shots for a new shooter on flying targets should be taken from a position of "slow, straight away."

Not only will the child experience a greater degree of success by having a relatively easier target to shoot at, there will be less of a chance of a safety violation or accidents when the barrel is pointed straight down range rather than swinging across an arc.

I use a trap whose spring can be adjusted to a low setting and whose angle and degree of motion can be easily adjusted with the turn of a few screws.

We have a very brief conversation on the movement of the barrel to and across the clay and when to pull the trigger, as well as a quick safety reminder of what to do if they are unprepared or if there is any type of misfire or malfunction of the firearm.

After several sessions with success, you will be able to move the child on to more complicated shots such as quartering away, crossing left to right, incoming, etc.

Shotgunning and shotgun competition sports are a very exciting event for children to participate in. While shooting with a hand trap in an open field can make for a great deal of fun, your local range likely offers one of the following shotgun games for a small fee.

All are scored games, which will introduce competition upon participation.

TRAPSHOOTING

Often referred to simply as "trap," trapshooting is one of and the most common of the three major competitive clay target shotgun sports.

Participants stand at one of several stations behind a "house" from which the clay target his throne. The participant fires five shots from each station on the line for a total of 25 shots per round.

After each series of five shots, in succession among the participants, the

Many kids enjoy trapshooting, and with the growing participation in the Scholastic Clay Target Program, it can even be a varsity-level sport!

shooter rotates to the next station. By doing so, the participant experiences differences in the angle and elevation of shots from not only the position of the target thrower, but from their position behind the target at the different stations as well.

Trapshooting has become rather popular, especially with the introduction of the scholastic clay target program – a program that promotes gun safety, personal responsibility and sportsmanship for both primary and secondary school students (usually ages 10 to 18). More and more high schools are offering trap shooting through the scholastic clay target program as a varsity–level sport, with sponsorship by state athletic associations, as well as credentials to earn varsity letters while in school. There are many colleges now that offer shooting scholarships and shotgun competition at the local, regional and even national level.

SKEET SHOOTING

I am not a big fan of skeet shooting for beginning shooters, due to the many different variables. As your shooter advances and proves proficient with all safety rules and other clay games, skeet can be a fun introduction, though.

In skeet shooting, the shooter shoots at 25 targets that are shot from eight different positions on a semi-circle that is a little more than 20 yards across.

Targets are thrown from two different stations – a "high" house on the left side of the course and a "low" house on the right side of the course.

While all clay target shooting is meant as a simulation of hunting different birds, skeet was the first to use so many different angles.

At certain stations the shooter will shoot a single bird from each house, and at others will need to shoot doubles – targets both thrown at the same time. In skeet, the variation is only from where you stand at the different positions on the course. Each clay target is thrown to the exact same point on every throw. They do not vary unless affected by outside forces such as wind or rain.

SPORTING CLAYS

Sporting clays is the shooting sport that most closely mimics actual, hunting shot situations. Locations, angles, size of target, direction and even obstacles all change with each station. Some courses even mix in different colored targets as "non-targets"- i.e. the shooter is penalized if they shoot at and break it.

Sporting clays is an excellent sport to introduce youngsters who wish to hunt to the different variables, safety issues, and even safe handling of a shotgun before they are actually brought into the field.

Often described as "golf with a shotgun," sporting clays courses take up a great deal more land space than either trap or skeet ranges do, and are usually at least 30 to 40 acres in size.

The typical sporting clays course consists of 10 to 15 different stations, with each station having a different presentation of the shot situation. Many have names that allude to what they are trying to mimic. "Springing teal" is two clays thrown straight up into the air from a hidden trap. "Flushing grouse" are usually thrown out at an obscure angle and shot through gaps in a wooded area of the course. There are even special clay targets designed to be rolled along the ground to simulate a bounding rabbit.

Targets are thrown as singles, true pairs (where two clays are thrown at the same time); following pairs (where one bird is thrown followed by a one- or two-second delay and then another clay is thrown); and report pairs, where the second clay is thrown immediately after shooting the first.

Courses are scored on either 50 or 100 targets.

Sporting clays also takes up a great deal more time for a round, given the number of shots and the distance the shooter must travel between stations to complete the course.

YOUTH FIREARM COMPETITION RESOURCES

THE CIVILIAN MARKSMANSHIP PROGRAM

Competitive marksmanship is a large part of the Civilian Marksmanship Program's mission. It is their belief that competition reinforces firearms safety and enables competitors to further develop their marksmanship skills and in many cases, even earn recognition for doing so (including things like Olympic medals and college scholarships). On their website you will find news and descriptions of upcoming matches, how to enter them and more information on course of fire and what you can expect from your participation.

If you are new to competitive shooting, the Civilian Marksmanship Program and its affiliated clubs and organizations continually sponsor clinics and workshops to help get you/your child up to speed. The CMP highly recommends participating in the CMP – USAMU Small Arms Firing School for pistol and/or rifle during the National Matches at Camp Perry, Ohio. By completing one of their one- or two-day schools, you will learn the fundamentals of firearms safety and marksmanship, as well as have an introduction to one of the largest firearm competitions in the world.

Visit their site at http://thecmp.org.

THE SCHOLASTIC SHOOTING SPORTS FOUNDATION

This is a good program if your child is of elementary through high school age and wants to learn shotgun or handgun shooting, or maybe they are just curious about something that some of their friends have talked about... shooting guns! The Scholastic Clay Target Program (SCTP) and Scholastic Pistol Program (SPP) provide a safe, supervised environment to participate in shooting directly with their peers. The organization holds local, regional, state and national level competitions in trap, skeet and pistol.

Visit their site at http://sssfonline.org.

THE WINCHESTER/NRA MARKSMANSHIP QUALIFICATION PROGRAM

This is another excellent program through the NRA that encourages "self-competition" via scored targets that are sent in and then given rank accordingly through several designated skill levels, "Pro-Marksman" through "Distinguished Expert."

Relevant introductory qualifications are available in handgun, hunter marksmanship, muzzleloader, trap, skeet, and sporting clays, recreational clay target shooting, tactical rifle, high power rifle, 4-position rifle, rimfire rifle, smallbore rifle and air rifle qualification. Advanced shooting qualifications are also available.

The following is from NRA's Website, www.mqp.nra.org:

From a young shooter's first BB gun to sophisticated air rifles, shotguns, muzzleloaders, pistols and rifles, the Winchester/NRA Marksmanship Qualification Program offers family fun and enjoyment that can last a lifetime.

Qualification shooting is an informal, year-round recreational shooting activity that provides incentive awards for developing and improving marksmanship skills. It's a drill. We set the standards; you meet the challenge! Progression is self-paced and scores are challenging but attainable. Performance is measured against established par scores and any shooter who meets or exceeds those scores is entitled to the corresponding recognition awards for that rating. It's an honor system!

Shooters acquire the large discipline patch at the onset of the program and as each rating is earned, they are entitled to all of the corresponding awards for the rating. Each rating level has a skill rocker, medal and certificate award that recognizes and highlights the achievement.

The courses of fire in the qualification program are designed to take shooters from beginning skill levels (Pro-Marksman, Marksman) through intermediate levels (Marksman 1st Class, Sharpshooter, Expert) up to a nationally recognized skill level -- Distinguished Expert -- the pinnacle of the program. By the time a shooter completes the Distinguished Expert rating, he or she has attained a proficiency level paralleling that of a competitively classified Sharpshooter.

Qualification shooting can be conducted anywhere -- on public ranges, at your favorite club range, even on your own home range. BB and pellet gun shooters will find air gun qualification courses especially suited for informal home air gun ranges and family learning environments. Parents can shoot side by side with their children or start a neighborhood air gun shooting sports program for their children and their friends.

As you can see, competition can be a key factor in the introduction of youth to firearms, but it must be done properly to ensure that your sessions remain fun for the child and are done in a manner that enhances their learning of guns, rules and safety.

CHAPTER FIFTEEN

To Hunt or Not to Hunt, That is the Question...

©National Shooting Sports Foundation, Inc.

Opinions and definitions of hunting vary widely across the spectrum, and the topic often elicits strong emotional responses on both sides of the debate.

Merriam Webster's expanded encyclopedia definition of "hunting" states:

"Pursuit of game animals, principally as sport. To early humans hunting was a necessity, and it remained so in many societies until recently. The development of agriculture made hunting less necessary as a sole life support, but game was still pursued in order to protect crops, flocks, or herds, as well as for food. Weapons now commonly used in hunting include the rifle, shotgun, and the bow and arrow, and methods include stalking, still-hunting (lying in wait), tracking, driving, and calling. Dogs are sometimes employed to track, flush, or capture prey. In Europe, much of the land was owned by the aristocracy, and game-keepers were employed to regulate the amount of game that could be hunted in a given area. By the 1800s the land hunted upon was not or had never been privately owned, and there began to develop a "tragedy of the commons," in that no one hunter had any motive to limit the number of animals killed; certain species were hunted to, or very close to, extinction. To counter this development, ethical codes were established that give the quarry a fair chance to escape; attempts were made to minimize the suffering of wounded game; and game laws, licensing, and limited hunting seasons were established to protect game stocks. For instance, a modern license may authorize a hunter to kill only two deer during the brief season for deer, and he or she must present a kill to a game warden who will then document and tag the animal. There are often penalties and fines for being found with an animal that is not so marked."

Contrast that with Wikipedia's definition:

"Hunting is the practice of killing or trapping any living organism, or pursuing it with the intent of doing so. Hunting wildlife or feral animals is most commonly done by humans for food, recreation, or trade. In present-day use, lawful hunting is distinguished from poaching, which is the illegal killing, trapping or capture of the hunted species. The species that are hunted are referred to as game and are usually mammals and birds."

Hunting can also be a means of pest control. Hunting advocates also state that hunting can be a necessary component of modern wildlife management, to help maintain a population of healthy animals within an environment's ecological carrying capacity when natural checks such as predators are absent. However, hunting has also heavily contributed to the endangerment, extirpation and extinction of many animals.

The pursuit, capture and release, or capture for food of fish is called fishing, which is not commonly categorized as a form of hunting. It is also not considered hunting to pursue animals without intent to kill them, as in wildlife photography or birdwatching. The practice of foraging or gathering materials from plants and mushrooms is also considered separate.

Skillful tracking and acquisition of an elusive target has caused the word hunt to be used in the vernacular as a metaphor, as in treasure hunting, bargain hunting, and even hunting down corruption and waste.

Removing all emotion from the definition, hunting for the purpose of our discussion refers to the outdoor pursuit of any defined, legal game species by legal methods of fair chase with the intent of reducing to possession said game such that it may be properly utilized.

The difference between hunting and other outdoor recreational activities such as wildlife photography is that part of the process of hunting is the end of life of the animal. This is the reason that we use firearms and/or other weapons like bows.

You may stalk animals in order to get closer to them. You may observe ani-

Many kids take their experience with safe handling and use of firearms and move on to hunting, but many don't. How and why they choose is what is important.

mals from a close distance for an extended period. You may even photograph an animal to preserve its image and likeness, but in order to hunt, it is required that you take an animal's life.

One of my favorite quotes on hunting comes from Jose Ortega y Gasset's *Meditations on Hunting*: "One does not hunt in order to kill; on the contrary, one kills in order to have hunted...If one were to present the sportsman with the death of the animal as a gift he would refuse it. What he is after is having to win it, to conquer the surly brute through his own effort and skill with all the extras that this carries with it: the immersion in the countryside, the healthfulness of the exercise, the distraction from his job."

It is a very personal choice that some are encouraged and prepared to make, while others are most certainly not. For me, this was an easy choice. I grew up in a family where my father hunted avidly, all of his friends were hunters, and I wanted nothing more than to be just like my dad and them. When I was young, it did not occur to me that shooting was in and of itself a sport. It was something that you did in order to hunt.

Growing up, shooting was something that we did in order to hunt. When you come from a hunting family, the decision whether or not to hunt may happen even before you learn to shoot.

Hunting allows a youngster to experience a direct connection to their food.

Hunting is a very personal choice. There are many benefits to your child taking up the sport of hunting, not the least of which is being involved and more closely connected to both their food and nature. Hunting is a very active pastime, and an excellent form of exercise.

Some people, like me, are driven to participate by an underlying, overwhelming desire to do so. Others could take it or leave it. Finally, there are those who fall to the opposite end of the spectrum and not only do not wish to participate, but are against the sport.

I know several elite-caliber shooters who do not hunt, and who have told me that they can't bring themselves to shoot an animal. It does not in any way diminish their love of shooting.

Your experience, and your child's introduction, may be similar to one of the following examples, but most likely will be some combination of several.

I will address three perspectives on hunting… one from an avid hunter point of view, one from a casual outdoor family, and one from a non-hunter's perspective.

If you come from a hunting family, the question of whether or not your child chooses to hunt will most likely be an easy choice. Your child has most likely been introduced to wild game in various stages: fully furred and feathered, rendered for cooking, and served as table fare. There are several things, however, that you should be sure to keep in mind when you introduce your child and new shooter to hunting.

First, remember to keep hunting fun. Just like when you introduce them to the gun for the first time, a first experience hunting needs to be brought about in a friendly, easy-going, comfortable manner.

A child's first experience hunting should not be in a goose pit in frozen sleet and sub-freezing temperatures for six hours. When you are introducing your child to hunting, and your child experiences a desire to go, it becomes all about the child and not at all about you.

When it comes to a first hunting experience, there are two types of hunts that I recommend overwhelmingly. Those are a dove hunt or a squirrel hunt, and which hunt you choose may depend on what type of firearm your child has been introduced to and has some experience with.

DOVE HUNTING

Dove season in most areas begins in mid to late August or early September. In many states, the dove season has a noon opener for opening day. There are two huge advantages to this when it comes to introducing young children. First, it means that they do not have to wake up early, get ready in the dark and be tired for most of the day

Second, the weather is warm, so the child will remain relatively comfortable throughout the day. Be sure to bring some of their favorite soft drinks, etc. and perhaps even something to occupy them like a book (or, yes, even a handheld videogame) for any time the action slows.

If your child has been introduced to a shotgun already, you may want to bring it along and allow them to either participate for a short time with your immediate supervision (meaning you do not shoot) or, if you are hunting in a group where that is otherwise non-feasible, you can take a break and let them shoot at some empty hulls placed on tree branches.

Remember, just as in your introduction to firearms, this introduction to hunting should be more about the child than you, and you need to ensure experience remains fun for the entire time.

Your child will let you know when it is time to go, and I urge you to, no matter how good the shooting maybe, heed their call and possibly even go do something else fun and entertaining with them.

SQUIRREL HUNTING

Squirrel hunting is another enjoyable experience for young children. It shares many of the same advantages of dove hunting, as the season starts early in late summer or early fall, the weather is warm and participation is a relatively non-stressful and non-intensive experience.

There are two methods for squirrel hunting. The first method is to quietly sneak in to a stand of hardwood trees. This means you are looking for oaks, hickories, beach trees, etc. – anything that produces a desirable nut and food source for squirrels.

Sit together, quietly, at the base of a large tree and either wait and observe, or use a squirrel call that can be purchased at any major sporting goods stores or even most big-box stores that carry sporting goods.

Have the child try to spot the squirrel coming in. You may quietly direct their vision, but remaining still is one of the requirements for this type of hunting. That can pose a challenge to a child that seems to have "ants in their pants" most of the time. Fortunately, you can also hunt squirrels by spotting and stalking them in the same types of hardwood stands. Move slowly and cautiously, and look for movement both on the ground and in the trees.

In early season, a small-gauge shotgun such as a .410 or 20-gauge is ideal for spotting and stalking, as many of the shots you take will be on a moving animal.

For stand hunting, where you are sitting still, a bolt-action or semi-auto .22-caliber rifle is an ideal weapon choice. This also allows you to have the child participate, and even harvest their first game animal.

Another big advantage to squirrel hunting is that many of the habits and requirements in order to bag squirrels transfer to other types of hunting.

For the majority of the country, the whitetailed deer is the number one big game animal that is pursued. The two main methods of whitetailed deer hunting are still-hunting (sitting on the stand in a desirable habitat area), and spotting and stalking.

By the time your child is ready for big game hunting, they will already have a great deal of the experience and skill set in order to be successful.

Plus, let's face it… having action or doing something, especially for a young child, is always more fun than sitting for long periods of time.

If your family has a casual outdoor attitude and your child expresses a desire to try hunting, you have a choice to make. You can take them yourself, or you can set them up with an outdoor mentor. That person can be a relative, a friend or one of the several groups that specialize in those types of things. Two that I recommend are the United Sportsmen's Youth Foundation (www.USYF.com) or "Pass it On" Outdoor Mentors (www.outdoormentors.org). You can also find beginning hunter programs through the International Hunter Education Association, at www.IHEA.org.

INTRODUCING TWEENS AND TEENS TO HUNTING

As children get older, some of their friends and peers may already be involved in outdoor pursuits such as hunting. If they have limited to no experi-

In most states, there are early seasons that allow youth to hunt before the regular season opens. Conditions tend to be milder and there tends to be a greater chance for success, as the chosen species has not been pursued for many months.

ence hunting, you may want to take them on an introductory hunt as previously described for doves or squirrels. Manny, however, will want to participate in the same types of activities as their friends – and that can work out well, also.

The most popular types of hunting in the United States are deer hunting, upland bird hunting and waterfowl hunting.

Some excellent news for the new or inexperienced hunter or shooter is that many states offer special "youth hunting seasons" and even "youth hunting programs" (usually available for a minimal fee and run by volunteers). These programs are most often held prior to the regular hunting seasons, meaning that the weather is generally more temperate and odds of success are higher, as the chosen game has not been exposed to any pursuit for the majority of the year.

The only youth upland hunting season that I am aware of is a youth turkey hunt. Turkeys can be very exciting to hunt, but, unless the mentor knows what they are doing and how to call, can also be exceptionally frustrating.

If your child would like to turkey hunt, but you are not a skilled turkey hunter, I urge you to get in contact with someone at the National Wild Turkey Federation (www.NWTF.org) who can put you in contact with a mentor for your state's youth season.

Waterfowl hunting, while a great deal of fun, usually requires a special skill set, some specialized gear (boats, decoys) and the ability to blow a duck or

If you are not skilled in waterfowl hunting, the fine folks at Ducks Unlimited can connect you with a mentor for your state's youth waterfowl season.

A youngster's first deer is a memory that they will cherish forever.

goose call. If you are not skilled in waterfowl hunting, the fine folks at Ducks Unlimited (www.ducks.org) can connect you with a mentor for your state's youth waterfowl season.

Deer hunting is another story. The most fortunate thing about the United States is we have a very large amount of public land, much of which is open to hunting. In order to hunt deer, the equipment is rather minimal. You basically need only the proper safety clothing and an adequate firearm capable of harvesting a deer.

Certainly, there are many skills needed to be an effective and successful deer hunter, but you can have many enjoyable experiences with your child in the woods with a minimum of additional expense and acquired skill.

Regardless of what type of hunting your child chooses to participate in, remember that whenever we are handling or using a firearm we adhere to the 10 Commandments of firearm safety.

Finally, if you come from a non-hunting family, you have a fantastic opportunity in front of you. If you do not hunt and your child expresses the desire to try hunting, what a great opportunity for additional bonding time with your child! You can take the hunter safety course with them, participate in some beginning hunter programs by their side, and grow a strong, lifelong bond with your child.

If you do not wish to begin this journey alongside your child, that is fine. Many organizations out there, including those listed above, can help you find a great outdoor mentor to take them hunting and introduce them to a hobby they

If you take the right steps in introducing your child to firearms and hunting, you will have a partner in the outdoors for life.

can participate in for the rest of their lives

I really don't have a lot of advice for people in anti-hunting families, except to encourage you to support your child in exploring the types of activities and pursuits that they wish to, provided they are legal and safe.

HUNTER EDUCATION PROGRAMS AND REQUIREMENTS

Each state requires new hunters (or, more accurately, all new hunters born after a certain date) to attend and complete a hunter safety course. Many of these courses are held at local sporting clubs, sporting goods stores or firearm ranges. Part of the curriculum is learning the different components of and firing a gun. This makes an excellent way to introduce your child to both guns and hunting. Many parents choose to take the course with their child.

Due to the increasing popularity of hunting, and, unfortunately, to a shortage of volunteers to teach these courses, many courses fill up very early. Some hunter safety courses have as much as a six-month waiting list.

There is now another option that uses a technological solution to overcome the limited number of classroom seats available. That solution is HunterEdcourse.com

By navigating to the website www.HunterEdCourse.com, entering some basic information and paying a minimal fee (at the time of the printing of this book the course fee was $13, the lowest fee of any of the online hunting education courses), your child (and you) can complete the entire classroom training portion of the hunter education course at your own pace. The total estimated time to complete the course is between four and six hours.

This is the consistent, state mandate for all hunter safety courses, so regardless of where you take your course or how you complete it (online or in person), plan on spending between four and six hours in a classroom or online learning environment.

Note: many states also require you to compete a "field day" where you will take a written exam and be put through a field test in order to demonstrate your knowledge of the subject matter as well as safe firearm handling.

Be sure to schedule your field day and obtain your state certification in hunter safety before heading out to hunt.

CHAPTER SIXTEEN

Refreshers, Reminders and Reinforcements

©National Shooting Sports Foundation, Inc.

There is so much information to convey, so many variables, and so many details to take into account when introducing children to firearms. Let's review some of the key takeaways that we have learned about the proper introduction of youth to firearms.

In **Chapter 1**, we discussed why every child needs to learn about firearm safety – that it is important not only to expose children to new things and information, but is the responsible and ethical thing for us to do in order to keep all children safe.

Chapter 2 discussed when a child is old enough to be introduced to firearms. The short answer is that it is entirely dependent upon the child.

Chapter 3 had important tips and tricks for preparing to introduce young children to guns: Make certain you are familiar with the rules of safety and handling, create fun situations in which to learn and be consistent. The theme of this chapter was the role of fun and play in teaching young children. There was important information for teaching children of every age, dealing with left- and right-handed students as well as eye dominance.

Variables to consider when teaching kids include left- and right-handedness, and eye dominance.

Chapter 4 discussed tweens and some of the unique issues of teaching children ages 10 to 12. It also dispels the myth that there is a "magic age" that a child is ready to learn to shoot. Competition becomes an effective teaching and learning tool at this age.

Chapter 5 gave some helpful tips and tricks when dealing with teenagers. Teens tend to have issues that are more "adult-like" than younger children.

Chapter 6 discussed how video games can help and hurt, appropriately following the teen chapter. As with all things in life, responsible use and moderation is the most effective method in using video games as a reinforcement or teaching tool.

Chapter 7 discussed the 10 Commandments – the extension on the four cardinal rules of firearm safety. The 10 Commandments are:

Always treat every firearm as if it were loaded.

Always keep the muzzle pointed in a safe direction.

Keep your finger off the trigger until you are ready to shoot.

Be certain of your target and what lies beyond it.

Always keep your gun unloaded until ready to use.

Know how to use and operate your firearm safely.

Always wear proper I am your protection whenever you will be shooting.

NEVER use alcohol, prescription, or nonprescription drugs before or while shooting.

Use only the correct improper ammunition for your firearm.

Never rely on a gun safety as anything but a back up to your safe handling.

Chapter 8 discussed the concept of homework and provided specific exercises, questions and drills to reinforce what a child learns while under your instruction, and to encourage the development of good and safe habits when handling firearms.

Chapter 9 was all about choosing the right equipment and ancillary products to ensure safe, comfortable and fun experience when handling and shooting firearms. The key takeaway from this chapter is the concept of fit–feel–function in choosing a firearm and accessories for a child. Equipment that does not fit well, or is designed for a child of larger or smaller stature, is unsafe.

Chapter 10 described the demonstration of power that is mentioned in several areas of the book. This is an essential part of introducing any youth to firearms, as it makes a real impression of what a firearm, even a small one, is capable of doing and why we always, always, always follow the 10 Commandments of firearm safety.

Chapter 11 was all about putting deadly power in the hands of a child, and dealt mostly with responsibility – a very subjective assessment, and something that is different for every child. There were four key evaluators that you should

Choosing the right equipment helps ensure a safe, comfortable and enjoyable experience when handling and shooting firearms.

use prior to allowing a child to shoot – their level of knowledge of firearms and firearm safety, their openness to instruction, their interaction with and around others and their behavior. Use this knowledge to develop an effective plan to mentor that child in the safe handling and use of firearms.

Chapter 12 dives deeper into the 10 Commandments, and specifically focuses on the one rule that is never violated. It is the first rule of firearm safety – always treat every gun as if it were loaded – and following it ensures that you or students will never have an unfortunate incident with a firearm.

Chapter 13 dealt with your child's friends, neighbors, teachers and relatives. The topic of firearms is a delicate issue, one that a child needs to be properly prepared for in order to have a positive experience when facing potentially adverse or even confrontational experiences.

Chapter 14 introduced competition and some of the more popular shooting sports available to youth, as well as the benefits of competition, interaction with other youth their age, and additional instruction opportunities available.

Chapter 15 discussed hunting, whether your child should or shouldn't hunt and some hints and tips to make an introduction to the sport a positive, fun experience.

An introduction to hunting should be a positive, enjoyable experience.

SO, ARE YOU READY?

By now you should be well on your way to becoming an effective mentor to your child or any other youth you wish to introduce to firearm safety and safe use.

I leave you with this: The fact that you are reading this book says two things very clearly. You care about the safety and future of youth in this country, and you have an interest at least in shooting and firearms.

Our children are our future and I urge you to take the knowledge you have gained from this book and use it to become an advocate for the safe introduction and, hopefully, continued participation in firearm ownership and use by those you mentor. If we wish to continue the pursuit of happiness and freedom that we have today, it is our duty to instill within them the morals, ethics and values with which we have been raised.

As you read this book, our right to possess firearms in this country has been and remains to be under assault. As a nation "of the people, by the people, and for the people," the future of firearms and firearm ownership in the United States is up to you.

Regardless of your political affiliations, I urge you to become educated on important topics to our society and freedom, from people that you associate with, as well as several, competing viewpoints, and then make sure to take part in our political process by voting your conscience based on that thorough education.

Good shooting,

Ace

CHAPTER SEVENTEEN

Additional Resources, Information and Links

©National Shooting Sports Foundation, Inc.

THE NATIONAL RIFLE ASSOCIATION

The following is from the NRA website:

Dismayed by the lack of marksmanship shown by their troops, Union veterans Col. William C. Church and Gen. George Wingate formed the National Rifle Association in 1871. The primary goal of the association would be to "promote and encourage rifle shooting on a scientific basis," according to a magazine editorial written by Church.

After being granted a charter by the state of New York on November 17, 1871, the NRA was founded. Civil War Gen. Ambrose Burnside, who was also the former governor of Rhode Island and a U.S. senator, became the fledgling NRA's first president.

An important facet of the NRA's creation was the development of a practice ground. In 1872, with financial help from New York State, a site on Long Island, the Creed Farm, was purchased for the purpose of building a rifle range. Named Creedmoor, the range opened a year later, and it was there that the first annual matches were held.

Political opposition to the promotion of marksmanship in New York forced the NRA to find a new home for its range. In 1892, Creedmoor was deeded back to the state and NRA's matches moved to Sea Girt, New Jersey.

The NRA's interest in promoting the shooting sports among America's youth began in 1903 when NRA Secretary Albert S. Jones urged the establishment of rifle clubs at all major colleges, universities and military academies. By 1906, NRA's youth program was in full swing with more than 200 boys competing in matches at Sea Girt that summer. Today, youth programs are still a cornerstone of the NRA, with more than one million youth participating in NRA shooting sports events and affiliated programs with groups such as 4-H, the Boy Scouts of America, the American Legion, Royal Rangers, National High School Rodeo Association and others.

Due to the overwhelming growth of NRA's shooting programs, a new range was needed. Gen. Ammon B. Crichfield, adjutant general of Ohio, had begun construction of a new shooting facility on the shores of Lake Erie, 45 miles east of Toledo, Ohio. Camp Perry became the home of the annual National Matches, which have been the benchmark for excellence in marksmanship ever since. With nearly 6,000 people competing annually in pistol, smallbore and high-power events, the National Matches are one of the biggest sporting events held in the country today.

The NRA is the largest and most extensive organization when it comes to firearms and shooting, and most all other programs have at least an "indirect" link via support, materials and material development, and firearm safety rules/tips developed over 150 years.

The NRA is the sanctioning body for hundreds of competitions every year for people of all ages, and is an organization that I urge you to explore it if you wish to be a responsible gun owner and citizen.

I have been a life member since 1988 and believe, along with millions of others, that the "first civil rights organization, ever" deserves its place atop the shooting and firearm world.

Key programs available through the NRA:

Training department: From the NRA Website: "From beginner to developing competitor, the NRA Training Department develops safe, ethical, responsible shooters through a network of more than 97,000 instructors and range safety officers, more than 5,700 coaches, and more than 1,800 training counselors. NRA Training Counselors recruit and train instructors to teach NRA's basic firearm courses. NRA Coaches, in turn, develop competitors at the club, high school, collegiate and national levels"

Eddie Eagle Program: The Eddie Eagle Program is a Non-shooting youth education and safety program that teaches pre-K through third grade children that is you find a firearm you should:

1. STOP!
2. DON'T TOUCH!
3. LEAVE THE AREA!
4. TELL A GROWNUP!

Over 26 million children have completed the program.

Various youth-oriented courses, competitions and resources can be found by visiting www.youth.nra.org.

Hundreds of books, pamphlets, courses, manuals, etc. on everything firearm and firearm-related can be found by visiting https://materials.nrahq.org.

THE NATIONAL SHOOTING SPORTS FOUNDATION
www.nssf.org

NSSF'S PROJECT CHILDSAFE

A fantastic and FREE resource for firearm owners, Project ChildSafe is a nationwide program that has been developed and implemented by the National Shooting Sports Foundation that promotes safe firearms handling and storage practices among all firearm owners through the distribution of safety education messages and free firearm Safety Kits.

These kits include a cable-style gun-locking device and a brochure (also available in Spanish) that discusses safe handling and storage. Since 2003, the project has partnered with local law enforcement agencies to distribute more than 36 million safety kits to gun owners in all 50 states and five U.S. territories.

Project ChildSafe's success is attributable to law enforcement, elected officials, community leaders, state agencies, businesses, the firearms industry and individuals who have worked to help raise awareness about the importance of securely storing firearms in the home.

NSSF'S WWW.WHERETOSHOOT.ORG

One of the most challenging aspects of introducing new shooters to both firearms and the shooting sports is finding a place to do it. The NSSF has compiled the most comprehensive, state-by-state list of places to shoot anywhere. In addition, you can find links to the NSSF's YouTube channel, where you can find hundreds of videos on everything from how to sight in a rifle to techniques on becoming a better shooter.

NSSF FIRSTSHOTS PROGRAM

If you don't have a great deal of experience with firearms, or maybe you know a lot about .22 rifles, but, say, nothing about shotguns, you may benefit from taking part in one of NSSF's "First Shots" programs. From the First Shots website: "First Shots has helped ranges across the country introduce thousands of individuals to shooting and firearm safety. Developed by the National Shooting Sports Foundation and hosted by independent shooting facilities, the program provides participants with a comprehensive introduction to shooting by qualified range operators and instructors that includes firearm safety, local ownership requirements, shooting fundamentals, hands-on instruction and how and where to continue."

Visit www.nssf.org/FirstShots to find out more information about these and other new shooter program.

THE SCHOLASTIC SHOOTING SPORTS FOUNDATION
www.sssfonline.org

If your child is of elementary through high school age and wants to learn shotgun or handgun shooting, or maybe they are just curious about something that some of their friends have talked about − shooting guns − then the Scholastic Shooting Sports Foundation deserves your attention! The Scholastic Clay Target Program and Scholastic Pistol Programs provide a safe, supervised environment to participate in trap shooting, skeet shooting and pistol shooting directly with their peers.

Through a variety of fun, team-based shooting practice and tournaments in both the Scholastic Clay Target Program (SCTP) and Scholastic Pistol Program (SPP), the SSSF provides student athletes aged elementary through college with a supportive environment where shooting sports serve as catalysts for teaching life lessons and skills that emphasize positive character traits and citizenship values. Throughout all training, practice and competitions, they instill in all participants a commitment to safe firearm handling, teamwork and leadership.

The Scholastic Clay Target Program was originated by the National Shooting Sports Foundation, the trade association for the shooting, hunting and firearms industry, and adheres to their industry standards for safety and education. In 2007, NSSF spun off SCTP and the Scholastic Shooting Sports Foundation, Inc. was formed. As the parent organization, NSSF provides ongoing support of the SSSF mission. Whether youth target shooting, pistol target shooting or skeet and trap shooting, each of the team-based sports are coordinated by full-time national program directors, regional directors of development, volunteer state advisors, coaches and national staff ensuring that all students involved learn and grow safely.

THE UNITED SPORTSMEN'S YOUTH FOUNDATION
www.usyf.org

The United Sportsmen's Youth Foundation is a 501c(3) non-profit organization created to address a "disconnect" of children from the outdoors and agriculture through the increased urbanization of society. Unlike other agricultural-centered programs, the USYF works extensively with youth from urban and suburban, rather than rural environments. The mission of the USYF is:
- To teach children about conservation.
- To further work to unite sportsmen, agriculture and communities.
- To preserve land for youth education, particularly in areas of rapid development.
- To provide and preserve precious multi-use habitat for children.
- To provide outdoor learning center near schools.
- To teach children personal involvement can positively impact wildlife and habitat.
- To offer all youth an opportunity to participate in, and enjoy the great outdoors thru safe, responsible use.

A large portion of the USYF's curriculum involves the safe handling and shooting of firearms.

With 15 US-based chapters and five international chapters, this is an organization rapidly making a name for themselves in youth conservation and firearm education.

The USYF also acts as a catalyst for the youth programs of other organizations by assisting with facility acquirement, land use, event planning and youth event marketing.

Each year the United Sportsmen's Youth Foundation holds several "Youthfest" events across the country where youth and new shooters can experience an "all in one" location try-out of air rifles, .22 rifles, slingshots, archery and shotguns in the same day and absolutely FREE OF CHARGE thanks to their fundraising and the donations of sponsors such as Benelli USA, Truglo, ThermaCell, Limbsaver, Cabela's, Federal Ammunition, ShockEater, the NRA and numerous others.

From September through April, the USYF also sponsors several "Hunting Encounter" programs that include upland and waterfowl hunts in Illinois, Wisconsin and North Dakota that are free or exceptionally low cost.

CAMP COMPASS ACADEMY

Camp Compass Academy (CCA) is a non-profit, year round, after school program dedicated to enhancing the lives of urban youth. It is a mentoring system developed and driven by educators. Its success is due to the fact that no one understands the needs of children better than teachers. It is CCA's mission to provide a unified effort to introduce urban, middle and high school students to various outdoor activities. During these sessions students will be introduced and networked to community businesses and working role models. The consequence will be an educated and influenced population understanding conservation, sportsmen's philosophies and their activities.

A large portion of Camp Compass's curriculum involves the handling and firing of firearms in both target shooting and hunting situations with safe, adult supervision.

CCA provides students with opportunities not readily available to inner-city children. Students enrolled within CCA are provided with a multitude of resources and services to help them succeed in their daily lives. The educational framework for the CCA is based on a multi-layered system developed by the founder of the program, John Annoni. Students are exposed to each phase of the system throughout their career at CCA, which may span over six years. The system includes five levels: exposure, exploration, extension, effective application and example mentoring. With each level of the program, there are increasing amounts of support and services provided to the students. There are many individualized services provided by the CCA, which include the following: one-on-one tutoring, homework assistance, mentor assistance and encouragement, individual goals, healthy peer relations, self-esteem and test-taking skills. Students are rewarded based on improvements and successes in their academic careers. Students are exposed to outdoor excursions and trips as well as educational meetings designed to reflect the mission of the CCA organization. Voluntary teachers, family members, college interns, peer mentors, community advocates and students participants alike have worked hand-in-hand to help better the lives of the economically disadvantaged children.

Camp Compass Academy is a program which:
- Allows interaction between students and teachers beyond the classroom.
- Integrates adaptive Science, Math, Social Studies and English curriculum.
- Develops character and self esteem through student centered learning.
- Takes a proactive stance towards firearm education..
- Builds bridges between cultures, ages and socioeconomic status.
- Demonstrates conservation practices and environmental respect.
- Promotes a positive connection with the community.
- Offers community job links and student references.

CCA is dedicated to enriching the lives of the youth it serves. Students within the program attend weekly after school tutoring sessions as well as summer and winter break educational opportunities. It is at these locales that students receive tutoring and academic mentoring from trained volunteers and are also exposed to various community presentations and speakers about current events and interests.

NATIONAL WILD TURKEY FEDERATION JAKES "TAKE AIM" PROGRAM

From the NWTF Website:

The NWTF's JAKES Take Aim program was made possible by a generous donation from Larry and Brenda Potterfield, founders of MidwayUSA. The goal of the JAKES Take Aim program is to present opportunities for youth age 17 and younger to try target shooting, clay target shooting and shotgunning in a safe, fun environment.

This goal will be achieved through two programs.

Airgun Program

Each NWTF state chapter in the lower 48 states will receive a fully equipped airgun trailer to use during local JAKES and youth events. The trailer contains everything needed to set up an indoor or outdoor airgun range.

Shotgun Program

NWTF chapters, in partnership with local shooting ranges and gun clubs, can host sporting clay shooting events. The program will provide clay targets and ammunition for registered and approved events.

Each year NWTF chapters across the United States and Canada host JAKES (Juniors Acquiring Knowledge, Ethics and Sportsmanship) events to help pass on the traditions of responsible hunting, teach the principles of habitat management, hunting ethics and safety. Many JAKES events will incorporate the JAKES Take Aim airgun trailers.

DUCKS UNLIMITED GREENWING PROGRAM

The DU Greenwing program is specifically designed for younger children to learn about waterfowl, conservation and habitat preservation. With thousands of chapters across the country, many local Ducks Unlimited chapters hold special Greenwing educational events, many of which include safe handling and shooting of firearms.

PHEASANTS FOREVER

Pheasants Forever and Quail Forever's "Forever Shooting Sports" program is the organization's comprehensive shooting sports program. With the support of Pheasants Forever and Quail Forever chapters, as well as corporate partners, the Forever Shooting Sports program is an opportunity for youngsters to be safely introduced into the world of shooting and upland hunting...and a gateway into the world of upland conservation. The organization also offers sponsorship of youth shooting sports teams, endowment and sponsorship opportunities, and grants to offset the cost of ammunition, one of the highest costs in participation in the shooting sports.

www.pheasantsforever.org/Youth/Forever-Shooting-Sports

YOUR STATE DEPARTMENT OF NATURAL RESOURCES/ CONSERVATION DEPARTMENT

Each state has its own department of natural resources (sometimes referred to as the state conservation department) that has responsibility and authority for a multitude of different areas and divisions.

The state DNR is usually the main authority over a state's waterways, second only to the Coast Guard. They typically also acquire, develop maintain, protect and enforce state and, to an extent, federal laws on all state-owned, federal-owned, and even private land. The department of natural resources is also responsible for determining season lengths, bag limits and general hunting rules for the state.

Each department tends to have different divisions with multiple responsibilities that can become complex when trying to explain. In its most simple form, the state DNR is what protects, preserves, maintains and is the main enforcement body for laws regarding the lands of each state in this country. They also are responsible for the oversight and, quite often, the implementation of the hunter safety program in their respective states.

The easiest way to find your respective department of natural resources is to type "(your state) department of natural resources" into the search engine of your choice online.

OTHER HELPFUL INFORMATION AND LINKS

www.americanfirearms.org/manufacturers/ - Excellent resource list of firearm manufacturers that sell firearms in the United States

www.shootata.com - The Amateur Trapshooting Association serves as the governing body for the sport of American style trapshooting

State government websites: http://www.usa.gov/Agencies/State-and-Territories.shtml

POPULAR OUTDOOR AND SPORTING GOODS RETAILERS THAT SELL FIREARMS AND ACCESSORIES

Bass Pro Shops .... www.Basspro.com
Cabela's... www.Cabelas.com
Gander Mountain...................................... www.GanderMountain.com
Academy Sports and Outdoors.............. www.academy.com
Dicks Sporting Goods............................. www.dickssportinggoods.com
Dunham's Sports .... www.dunhamssports.com
WalMart .... www.WalMart.com
Scheels... www.Scheels.com
Sportsman's Warehouse .... www.Sportsmanswarehouse.com

RECOMMENDED AND POPULAR HUNTING AND SHOOTING PERIODICALS

Gun Digest .... www.gundigest.com
Outdoor Life Magazine .... www.outdoorlife.com
Field and Stream...................................... www.field andstream.com
Outdoor News.. www.outdoornews.com
Petersens Hunting.................................... www.petersenshunting.com
Wildfowl... www.wildfowl.com
Guns and Ammo .... www.gunsandammo.com

POPULAR FIREARM AUCTION AND INFORMATION WEBSITES

www.gundigest.com
www.Guns.com
www.Gunbroker.com
www.Ammoland.com
www.Cheaperthandirt.com
www.MidwayUSA.com
www.GunsAmerica.com
www.armslist.com
www.gunauction.com
www.gunsinternational.com

Acknowledgments

Without the effort and assistance of a great many people, this book would not have been possible. Some of that help has come in bits, fits and pieces over the course of my lifetime, while other portions have come during the compilation of this writing work.

The first special thanks goes to my beautiful wife, Valerie, without whom I would have very little direction, let alone passion and understanding. Valerie, your love and support makes the additional efforts worth it. It takes a special kind of person to understand the demands, travel schedules, benefits and drawbacks of being a high-level, executive salesperson, let alone a writer and outdoor professional. Your compassion, understanding, support, schedulekeeping and, most of all, flexibility, certainly have made my life and ability to do my job easier. You skillfully juggle the rules of homemaker, support person, secretary, chef, nurse, cleaning person, travel agent, taxi and shuttle service, "keeper of the realm" and personal cheerleader. When it really counts, you never disappoint. Finally, your beauty and pure heart still captivate and enchant me, and I love you more each day.

Special thanks go out to my parents, Jerry and Gail. Dad, without your passionate pursuit of hunting and shooting, as well as your patient introduction of me, and your grandchildren later on, to the wonderful world of guns and shooting, I would not be the man I am today. Thanks, Dad, for always taking me hunting. Mom, without your unconditional love and support over the years as well as your effort and wisdom, our family would not have the successful dynamic that we do. Additionally, who better to go to for a "teacher's perspective" than the best teacher I have ever known in 42 years?

Thank you to my children for their patient posing for thousands of pictures over their lives, sometimes for fun, and sometimes for "daddy's work…." I love you all so very, very much and I'm proud of each of you.

To my friend and mentor, Steve Sipress, I owe a great deal of my success in and out of the firearms world to the ideas that you profess, but specifically, that anyone can be an expert in anything- they just need the drive and desire. You lead by example to those of us in your mentorship, and we are indebted to you.

Thanks, Christy, for your legal expertise, and Gina for those important pictures. All was almost lost.

Thanks again, Chuck Fretwell, for helping out a new guy in the industry and opening doors that would've otherwise remain closed.

Thank you, Steve Hoffa, for being the catalyst that allowed me to pursue my passions as a career. Additionally, thank you for your help in obtaining pictures and the right copy for Cannon's fine products.

Thanks, Scott Dobry for giving a new guy a shot and for your help, tutelage, and continued friendship.

Thanks to my friends and colleagues on the "Best and largest networking group for outdoor professionals on LinkedIn," Hunting, Fishing, and Outdoor Professionals, for your help with topics, titles, ideas and, most importantly, proper photography to illustrate said topics. I promise to continue "paying it forward" through and with you.

There are people that you meet in life who you are immediately drawn to, and Dave Dolbee is certainly one of those. Thanks, Dave, for your friendship, your editorial advice, and for being a catalyst for one another in the hunting and shooting world. You can share my campfire any time.

Thank you to Brendan Walsh of the United Sportsmen's Youth Foundation, Mike Christiansen of Pass it On Outdoor Mentors, and John Annoni of Camp Compass not only for your assistance, but for the many things you do to help today's youth experience hunting, shooting and the outdoors. We need 10,000 more just like you!

In remembrance of Kay Hansen, my Sophomore English teacher, and a woman of tremendous faith in God, Catholic School and me. Thank you, Mrs. Hansen, for finding such a hidden talent. Before you allowed my creativity to flow, I loathed writing and never dreamed of the possibilities and career potential that it had. I will always remember the first piece you assigned me to prove that, "Why they call it hunting."

Finally, thanks again, Ed Cawley… the "Old Man" to this "Boy." I promised you to never quit, and I haven't. Your wisdom and tutelage live on through me, my children and all those whose lives you touched. We all miss you. I know that someday I will again be able to row boats, move decoys and "chouse" cover for you. I hope whomever has that job now is acceptable. Go maire sibh bhur saol nua, E.C.!

About the Author

JERRY "ACE" LUCIANO is a businessman, an entrepreneur, consultant, bestselling author, seminar speaker, Black Belt martial artist and consummate outdoorsman for over 30 years. He has travelled the globe in pursuit of both game and fish throughout the United States, Canada, Mexico, Africa, Europe and Australia.

For 20+ years, Ace has been involved in numerous conservation organizations and youth projects. In 1995 Ace was the youngest director ever elected to the board of directors of any Safari Club International chapter. The chapters that he helped to found have earned Rookie Chapter of the Year, Chapter of the Year, and Conservation Organization of the Year honors. He was instrumental in each of those chapters' youth events.

For the past 11+ years, Ace has been a founding and active member, an executive director, and state coordinator for the United Sportsmen's Youth Foundation, an organization that introduces youth to shooting, hunting, and the outdoors. Each year Ace runs several free youth events that introduce thousands of new shooters and hunters to the sport.

Most important of all, Ace is a father of four fantastic children, all of whom were introduced to and have been shooting from a very early age.

GUN
SAFETY
IN THE HOME

MASSAD AYOOB

This is an excerpt from the new Gun Digest book *Gun Safety in the Home*, by Massad Ayoob

CHAPTER ONE

CORE FIREARMS SAFETY PRINCIPLES

"The Devil loads the empty gun"
— Old Latin American saying

The firearm is defined at law as a lethal weapon. The hunter uses it as sporting equipment. The farmer uses it as a tool. The target shooter literally uses it as a remote control paper punch. And, from homeowners to police to military, many people carry them expressly because they are deadly weapons, the only effective tool that can ward off homicidal humans who have lethal capability of their own and are trying to murder the legitimate owners of those guns, or innocent victims within their mantle of protection.

We spend our lives surrounded by dangerous equipment. Automobiles. Anything electrical. Gasoline and countless other flammables and explosives, drain cleaner, powerful medications and countless other toxic substances. Power tools, of which the gun is one – in essence, an explosively operated drill that works from a distance.

We must use them all with the utmost care. We must be thoroughly familiar with their proper use. We are responsible for keeping them out of the hands of those who might do harm with them. That category includes unsupervised children, but also encompasses irresponsible or incompetent adults, and anyone who might intentionally use them to commit wrongful acts. This in turn encompasses protecting them from theft. A huge percentage of criminals who commit "gun crimes" do so with firearms stolen from the law-abiding. There are probably only two products thieves can steal from you that they can sell on the black market for more than their intrinsic value, instead of fencing them for pennies on the dollar: prescription drugs and deadly weapons.

Let's examine some well-established rules of firearms safety. The longest standing are "The Ten Commandments of Gun Safety." They have appeared in various forms over the generations. Here is a current version, from Remington Arms.

THE TEN COMMANDMENTS OF FIREARMS SAFETY
(from the Remington Arms website, www.remington.com)

- Always keep the muzzle pointed in a safe direction.
- Firearms should be unloaded when not actually in use.
- Don't rely on your gun's safety.
- Be sure of your target and what's beyond it.
- Use proper ammunition.
- If your gun fails to fire when the trigger is pulled, handle with care.
- Always wear eye and ear protection when shooting.
- Be sure the barrel is clear of obstructions before shooting.
- Don't alter or modify your gun and have it serviced regularly.
- Learn the mechanical and handling characteristics of the firearm you are using.

Now, let's look at each of those directives in more depth.

ALWAYS KEEP THE MUZZLE POINTED IN A SAFE DIRECTION

This will ideally mean that the gun is always pointed at something which can safely absorb the most powerful round that particular gun can fire. Up in the air when outdoors seems safe, but every year people are killed or injured by the foolish practice of celebratory gunfire, that is, firearms discharged upward like relatively harmless fireworks. A few years ago, a hunter emptied his muzzleloader at the end of a day afield by firing it skyward. The bullet came down a great distance away and struck in the head a teenage Amish girl in a horse-drawn buggy, killing her.

This element of gun safety is why other detectives get nervous when one investigator in the squad room is carrying his pistol in a horizontal shoulder holster: anyone standing behind him is in line with the muzzle. It is one reason why many shooters refuse to wear an appendix holster, which holds the muzzle of the gun in line with the genitalia and the femoral artery, particularly when the wearer is seated. A gun in a holster, if left alone, is most unlikely to become possessed by demons and fire by itself. However, I remember the off-duty cop in a crowded theater who said he was "adjusting" his pistol in its concealed shoulder holster when it discharged. Fortunately, nobody was hit by the bullet.

FIREARMS SHOULD BE UNLOADED WHEN NOT ACTUALLY IN USE

The gun being carried by a police officer or, for that matter, a private citizen with a carry permit, actually is in use, and so is the defensive firearm stored in a place of business or the home. That use is sentinel duty, emergency equipment ready to be immediately employed to save life.

DON'T RELY ON YOUR GUN'S SAFETY

Anything made by man can fail. I have seen semiautomatic pistols whose thumb safety was so out of adjustment that when the trigger was pulled, an observer could see the untouched safety lever appear to pull itself down from "safe" to "fire" position as the hammer fell and discharged the pistol.

This certainly should not be taken as advice to NOT use the manual safety, especially when the gun is carried loaded. We will never know how many people were saved from shooting themselves in the leg when the trigger caught a poorly designed safety strap or a coat's adjustment cord as it was being holstered, solely because an engaged manual safety kept the pistol from discharging when the trigger was "artificially pulled." We do know that there have been many, many cases where a criminal has gotten a gun away from a good guy, usually a cop, tried to shoot him with his own pistol, and failed because the criminal couldn't find the inconspicuous little safety lever that "turned the gun on." We'll never know how many hunters were saved in the woods when they were maneuvering through a thicket and a tree branch snapped inside the trigger guard, hard enough to discharge the gun, and the rifle or shotgun remained silent because the safety catch was engaged.

BE SURE OF YOUR TARGET AND WHAT'S BEYOND IT

In the south, a police officer shot at a poisonous snake in a tree. The bullet continued its flight, eventually coming down to strike a young boy far from the officer and out of his line of sight. Hunting videos exist where you can see a hunter aim at what appears to be a single antelope or hog, and fire. That animal falls, revealing an animal behind it that staggers and falls as well. Unseen by the hunter, it has been killed or wounded by a bullet passing through the intended target.

Always remember that on the range, shooting from a low position such as kneeling or prone may angle your shots upward, over the bullet-stopping back-stop or berm. Always take a careful line of sight before firing. Similarly, firing at targets on the ground midway between shooter and berm can cause bullets to ricochet on an angle that may allow them to escape the range with tragic results. One reason police and responsible homeowners and concealed carri-ers load their defensive firearms with hollow point bullets and similar rounds designed to stay inside the body of the offender is that this target is the only backstop they have. A projectile that pierces through and through the violent attacker may kill or cripple an innocent person behind him, blocked from the shooter's view by any number of things: distance, darkness, tunnel vision, a curtain or sheetrock wall, or the imposing bulk of the offender himself.

USE PROPER AMMUNITION

This writer was on the board of directors of a good-size gun club when called to respond to the range due to a gun blow-up. A member had been sighting in his two hunting rifles, a .308 and a .270. He was using the same brand of ammo, in similar packages, for both. He became so wrapped up in his shooting that when he reloaded his .270, he accidentally plucked .308 rounds from the other box and put them into the gun. The .308 Winchester cartridge is shorter than the .270 Winchester, so the bolt action closed on the live .308 round, the bullet tip of which was barely in the .270's chamber. However, the bullet was too wide for the bore – the inside of the barrel – and when he fired, pressure spiked and the gun blew up spectacularly. His face was badly cut, and because he was wearing flimsy sunglasses instead of proper eye protection, he suffered some permanent impair-ment of vision.

IF YOUR GUN FAILS TO FIRE WHEN
THE TRIGGER IS PULLED, HANDLE WITH CARE

The "hangfire," in which the cartridge fires a short time after its primer has been struck by the firing pin, is mostly seen with old-fashioned black powder guns, but can occur with modern ammunition at least in theory. In training for defensive emergencies, most of us will simply eject that cartridge and chamber another.

Far more dangerous, in this writer's opinion, is the gun that goes "poof" instead of "bang," or seems to have no recoil. If that happens, STOP! It is usually a signal that a weak round, called a squib, has just been fired. These will often lodge a bullet in the barrel. If another full power round is fired behind it, the resulting pressure spike will very likely explode the gun, causing serious injury or even death. Carefully remove all other ammunition from the gun, and run a cleaning rod or something similar down the barrel to check for obstructions.

ALWAYS WEAR EYE AND EAR PROTECTION WHEN SHOOTING

This also goes for anyone else on the range, whether they're shooting or not. Hearing damage from gunfire is cumulative, and serious hearing loss often does not show up for years. Audiologists tell me it is not reversible. I strongly suggest ear plugs *and* ear muffs, particularly with high powered rifles and loud Magnum handguns, and any other firearm with a particularly sharp, high-decibel report. Well-fitted plugs give the illusion of the same sound attenuation you get with good muffs, but audiologists tell us that

Keep your firearms well maintained and in good working order. This neglected 1911 pistol has obstructions in the bore that could make it dangerous to shoot.

much of the sound impulse which causes the high range nerve deafness we call shooter's ear comes by way of vibrations through the mastoid bone, against which plugs offer little or no protection. Muffs do shield that area. However, the stems of the safety glasses we must wear while shooting break the seal of the muffs at a critical juncture, allowing noise in. The plugs are a safety net to allow for that. Hence, plugs and muffs.

I'd urge you to invest in active hearing protectors, for reasons of safety as well as performance. Amplifying low sounds but reducing loud ones, these allow you to hear range commands. One of my fellow instructors was about to give a "fire" command to a line of shooters at a police range he'd been assured had nothing to harm behind the brush of the backstop, when he heard something in that brush through his enhanced muffs. He gave a cease fire command. Moments later, a mentally-challenged man wandered out of the brush where the officers had been about to unleash a fusillade that might well have killed him had the instructor not been wearing active hearing protectors.

Eye protection is critical, without it, this writer would have been totally blind before reaching voting age. One day in my early teens I was shooting a WWII surplus Czech .380 pistol. It had apparently been made late in the war with slave labor, sloppy or perhaps even sabotaged workmanship, and poor heat treating. A few shots into the shooting session, the firing pin retainer crystallized. On the next shot, the firing pin came straight back out of the gun, directly at my right eye. It would have skewered my eyeball through the pupil like a toothpick in a martini olive had it not been for my tempered eyeglasses, which were chipped and cracked by the violent impact. Not long after, I was shooting a cheap ($12.95) .22 Short revolver at a small steel bullet trap in my basement when, at the first shot – WHAM! Something struck me violently in the face, hard enough to knock my eyeglasses off. It turned out that the shoddy revolver had been assembled with the barrel screwed in off-thread, causing it to shoot far to the left. The low-powered .22 Short bullet had struck the reinforced outer edge of the bullet trap and come straight back. The left lens of my eyeglasses was cracked, but had stopped the bullet from excavating my eye socket.

Wear protective glasses while cleaning guns, too! Ace firearms instructor Bob Smith in Coeur d'Alene, Idaho, shows his students the cracked safety glasses he was wearing when he was taking apart an AK47, and one powerful spring got loose and came flying at him. The lens was ruined, but stopped the flying steel short of Bob's eye. The glasses serve other purposes in cleaning: I've been hit inadvertently in the eye with a shot of carbon tetrachloride-based gun cleaning spray, and it's a toss-up whether I'd rather do that again or take another training hit of OC pepper spray directly in the eyes.

BE SURE THE GUN BARREL IS CLEAR
OF OBSTRUCTIONS BEFORE SHOOTING

See above. I miss the plugged bottoms of the police holsters I wore in the years after I first pinned on a badge, and always preferred them for outdoorsman use. The reason is that something as simple as falling on your butt in snow or mud, or squatting in a snowdrift to examine a deer track, can inadvertently immerse the handgun's muzzle in muck or snow if the holster has an open bottom. The same is true of falling forward into such substances. Soldiers have learned to put masking tape or even condoms over the muzzles of their combat rifles for just this reason.

DON'T ALTER OR MODIFY YOUR GUN,
AND HAVE IT SERVICED REGULARLY

This rule bears some discussion. Most competitive shooters use guns modified for high performance, but are extremely careful to make sure they don't violate safety specs. With defensive firearms, it has become common in the legal world to falsely allege that a legitimate, deliberate self-defense shooting was actually negligent and unintended. There are several reasons for this. First, there is no such thing as a "justifiable accident." Second, in criminal court a politically-motivated prosecutor can much more easily convince the jury that a good guy got careless and made an indefensible mistake (manslaughter) than that he turned into a bad guy and killed with genuine malice (murder). Third, in a civil lawsuit, alleging that you the defendant shot his client deliberately shuts the plaintiff's lawyer out of the deep pockets of your insurance company, which only covers for negligence and is generally expressly exempt from having to pay for your having deliberately harmed that lawyer's client, a willful tort.

When opposing counsel is going in that direction and trying to show you to be reckless and negligent, you DON'T want to give him a weapon as powerful as "Ladies and gentlemen of the jury, this defendant DEACTIVATES THE SAFETY DEVICES ON LETHAL WEAPONS!!"

Similarly, "hair triggers" have long been associated with unintended discharges, and indeed have become a byword in the common parlance for people who "go off" when they shouldn't. A trigger pull of less weight than the manufacturer's specification for duty use is very deep quicksand in court. I've warned for years that the very light trigger pull is a two-edged sword. "The good news is, it's easy to shoot. The bad news is, it's easy to shoot."

LEARN THE MECHANICAL AND HANDLING CHARACTERISTICS OF THE FIREARM YOU ARE USING

Over the years, one problem we've seen is that novices – or people distracted, fatigued, confused, or terrified – perform functions out of sequence. The classic example with a firearm is that instead of unloading by removing the magazine and then clearing the firing chamber, they do that backwards. They clear the chamber, ejecting the round therein, and don't realize that they have just chambered another live round with the same action. They then remove the magazine and consider the gun empty, when in fact there's a live torpedo in the launch tube and when the trigger is pulled, the gun will fire. This has been known to end tragically.

It's important to know whether or not your gun is drop-safe, that is, whether it is capable of firing due to an inertia discharge if it is dropped on a hard surface, struck sharply, or subjected to the violent G-forces of a car crash. When in doubt, call the manufacturer, request the service department, and ask this specific question.

Long after the "Ten Commandments of Firearms Safety" became the standard, a WWII combat vet and master firearms instructor came along with something simplified, and geared specifically for defensive firearms. He was Lt. Col. Jeff Cooper, USMC (ret.), and his Four Rules have become a generic standard among modern gun people.

JEFF COOPER'S FOUR RULES

Col. Cooper's Four Rules were, in essence:

• Every gun is always loaded.

• Never allow the muzzle to point at anything you are not prepared to see destroyed.

   • Keep your finger out of the trigger guard until your sights are on target.

• Always be certain of your target and what is behind it.

COOPER'S RULE #1:
All guns are always loaded – or treated as carefully as if they were.

COOPER'S RULE #2: Never point the gun at anything you are not prepared to destroy. Here, pistol champ Gail Pepin, shooting right to left, strafes down a row of steel plates with her 9mm Glock.

COOPER'S RULE #3: Keep finger out of trigger guard until you are actually shooting, as demonstrated here.

COOPER'S RULE # 4: Always be certain of your target and what is behind it.

Cooper had brilliantly simplified the Ten Commandments for what another gun expert, Peter Kokalis, defined as Armed Professionals. It was understood they'd have guns they knew and the right ammunition. Even so, there are semanticists in every discipline, and the world of the gun is no exception. Let's take a quick, interpretive look at the Four Rules.

EVERY GUN IS ALWAYS LOADED

I don't believe the Colonel meant this literally. Would you walk into a gun show or even a gun shop if every firearm on display for handling were loaded?

I've visited the Colonel at his famous home, The Sconce, on the grounds of the Gunsite Training Center he created. Adorning the walls of his den were firearms he had made famous: his personal Bren Ten; the 8 3/8-inch barrel Smith & Wesson .44 Magnum he preferred for hunting; and the Browning Hi-Power in caliber .40 G&A that he had created with Whit Collins for the eponymous Guns & Ammo magazine, the journal in which he first earned fame. None of those guns were loaded when I saw them and examined them at his invitation. I believe what he was saying was simply, "Treat every gun as if it is loaded." It is widely known that unloaded guns cause the most tragedies, i.e., that foolish people do stupid things with them when they think they're incapable of harm.

NEVER POINT YOUR GUN AT ANYTHING YOU ARE NOT PREPARED TO DESTROY

In the world of firearms safety, wiser words were never spoken. This is why there should always be a safe backstop behind the aiming point even during dry fire. You always want every possible safety net. I explain to my students, "Look, I don't know you people yet, so until I do, don't point your guns at anything *I'm* not prepared to see destroyed, and we'll get along fine."

KEEP YOUR FINGER OUT OF THE TRIGGER GUARD UNTIL YOUR SIGHTS ARE ON TARGET

Often stated as "on target, on trigger; off target, off trigger," I respectfully suggest that this rule should go farther. It's fine for the shooting range, but in a danger situation where violent criminal suspects may be taken at gunpoint, at that moment the sights ARE on target and this interpretation of the rule would then put the finger on the trigger. Now, the person holding the gun is just one mishap away from accidentally killing a suspect who has surrendered to him and offered no harm.

Dr. Roger Enoka is the physiologist who has done the most comprehensive and ground-breaking work on physiology applied to accidental firearms discharges. He notes that several things may cause spasmodic, unintended discharges if the finger is on the trigger. These include startle response, whether the stimulus is a loud sound or an unexpected touch; interlimb response (in which the gun hand's fingers all tighten when the other hand closes, as when applying handcuffs); and postural disturbance, because when we lose our balance we instinctively clutch for something to hold us upright.

With that in mind, I would suggest this rule, one that I enforce at my own school: THE FINGER WILL ONLY BE INSIDE THE TRIGGER GUARD WHEN WE ARE IN THE VERY ACT OF INTENTIONALLY FIRING THE GUN!

Not "when we're ready to shoot." Hell, we should be ready to shoot when we put the gun on. Not "when we're on target." History shows that, for every time the trigger has to be pulled, cop and citizen alike will take many criminals at gunpoint and end matters with that act alone.

ALWAYS BE CERTAIN OF YOUR TARGET
AND WHAT IS BEHIND IT

I can't add much to that which hasn't been said elsewhere here.

It is sad that so many people use Col. Cooper's Four Rules without paying proper homage and crediting where they came from. That is a shame, because his work has undoubtedly saved more lives and more suffering than any of us will ever know.

AUTHOR'S SAFETY RULES

When you teach the gun, you're responsible for the safety of the students, the training staff, and of course, yourself. Here are the rules I've gone by for a very long time:

MASSAD AYOOB GROUP (MAG) SAFETY RULES: LIVE FIRE

First, the four core safety rules originally promulgated by Col. Jeff Cooper:

A: Treat every firearm as if it is fully loaded and ready to discharge.

B: Never point a firearm at anything you are not prepared to destroy.

C: Do not allow your trigger finger to be inside the trigger guard unless and until you are in the very act of intentionally firing the weapon.

D: Always be certain of your target and what is behind it.

When on a "cold range," gun will be unloaded at all times until you are instructed to load by instructor or range officer.

When manipulating the slide of a semiautomatic pistol, keep the muzzle downrange in a safe direction and do not allow hand, forearm, or other body parts to come in line with the muzzle. Retract the slide by grasping it at the rear, NOT from the front.

When unloading a semiautomatic pistol, remove magazine first and put it somewhere – pocket, pouch, or waistband – so support hand can be dedicated to slide manipulation, and primary hand can be dedicated to holding the gun in a safe direction, without either hand having to "juggle" the magazine.

When clearing the chamber of a semiautomatic pistol, allow the cartridge to fall to the ground and retrieve it later. Do NOT eject a live cartridge into the palm, or attempt to catch it in mid-air.

If you drop a gun, let it fall. Grabbing at a falling gun often results in unintentional pressure applied to the trigger, causing discharge in an uncontrollable direction.

When holstering any handgun, keep the trigger finger STRAIGHT outside the trigger guard, and use the thumb to safely keep single action auto's hammer from falling forward, or double action auto's hammer from rising and falling.

If your firearm malfunctions and you don't know how to clear it, keep it pointed downrange with the dominant hand and raise your support hand, which will summon a staff member to assist you.

Weapons are not to be handled after consumption of alcohol.

Advise staff (discreetly if you like) of any medical conditions, medications, etc. that may affect you while you are with us. If you are stricken, we need to know where your insulin/digitalis/etc. is.

IF YOUR MUZZLE CROSSES ANYONE INCLUDING YOURSELF – WHETHER OR NOT THE GUN IS LOADED – IT IS A SAFETY VIOLATION. THE MAG STAFF AND HOSTS RESERVE THE RIGHT TO REMOVE ANY SHOOTER FROM THE FIRING LINE FOR A SINGLE SAFETY VIOLATION, AND FOR THE REMAINDER OF THE DAY, THE STUDENT MAY OBSERVE BUT NO LONGER PARTICIPATE. HE OR SHE WILL RETURN TO THE LINE UNDER PROBATION (AND PARTICULAR SCRUTINY) THE FOLLOWING DAY. A SECOND SAFETY VIOLATION WILL RESULT IN THE STUDENT BEING IMMEDIATELY EXPELLED FROM THE PROGRAM, WITHOUT REFUND.

MASSAD AYOOB GROUP SAFETY RULES: DRY FIRE

Like virtually every training school, MAG recommends dry-fire practice to maintain manipulation skills. However, we have seen over the years that many unintended discharges occur in dry-fire, perhaps because "the empty gun" lulls the practitioner into complacency.

Follow the MAG live fire safety rules. These include, but are not limited to: treat every weapon as if it is loaded; never point it at anything you are not prepared to see destroyed; do not place your finger in the trigger guard until you are in the very act of intentionally pulling that trigger; and always be certain of your target and what is behind it.

Always check by sight and feel to confirm that the gun is in fact unloaded. THERE SHOULD BE NO LIVE AMMUNITION IN THE SAME ROOM WHERE YOU ARE PRACTICING DRY-FIRING.

Always aim the gun at something that can safely absorb the most powerful

The gentle hand of a coach is seen behind the shoulder of this new young shooter, to prevent too much muzzle rise as his Taurus 9mm recoils.

At Live Oak Police Department Teen Academy range day, Chief Buddy Williams explains S&W M&P15 .22 rifle and its magazine to students.

round that particular gun can fire÷because one day, it may indeed fire that round unexpectedly. Thickly packed bookshelves with no airspace, or cartons packed with books or magazines, serve nicely as dry fire backstops. So does body armor set against a wall, and the dedicated Safe Direction™ dry-fire backstop.

Never practice trigger-pulling and reloading in the same session. It is a good idea to not even practice them on the same day.

When practicing reloading, disable the gun. A field-stripped auto pistol with only frame, slide stop, and magazine(s) suffices for practice, and guarantees no shot can be fired. With a revolver, wrap a handkerchief or rag through the top-strap of the frame so the cylinder cannot be closed into firing battery. Opening and closing the cylinder is easy: getting the cartridges into the chambers is the hard part you want to work on.

When using dummy ammunition, take great pains to be sure that live ammo has not migrated into the "dummy cartridge" supply, and vice versa.

After a dry-fire session, do not reload and holster for street carry. Give mind and body time to absorb the fact that "draw gun, pull trigger" practice is OVER.

GUN-SPECIFIC SAFETY RULES

When I say gun-specific, I mean things specific to one or another type of firearm that go beyond general gun safety rules. Let's look at shotguns, rifles, and handguns.

SHOTGUNS

The shotgun is a particularly unforgiving weapon when its output strikes a human at close range. Treat it with great respect.

Ever since my young days at trap ranges, I've been horrified to see shotgunners "rest" their weapons with the muzzles on the top of their feet. Yes, the guns are unloaded and the actions are open, but it's still a grotesque violation of a prime directive, to wit, "Don't let the muzzle point at anything you are not prepared to destroy."

One thing to be careful with when working with these "scatterguns," is that a 20-gauge shotgun shell is so dimensioned that if it is inadvertently chambered in a 12 gauge barrel, it can slide down the inside of the barrel out of sight. As the barrel constricts, the rim of the shell comes to a stop. It appears to the shooter that the chamber is empty. Then, the time comes when a 12-gauge shell is loaded into the chamber and, eventually, fired.

Of course, the bore is blocked by the live 20-gauge shell that has been lying in wait. That obstruction by itself will constitute a pressure spike sufficient to blow up the gun. But, remember, that obstruction is a live shell full of gun powder of its own, and it has come to rest in a narrower part of the barrel which is not constructed to take the pressure of initial discharge. The combination blows up the gun, exploding the barrel at a point where the shooter's support hand is likely to be grasping the forend. The oral history of firearms safety is replete with amputated fingers and mangled or avulsed hands resulting from this kind of safety error.

Remember that most shotguns do not have internal firing pin safeties. Their

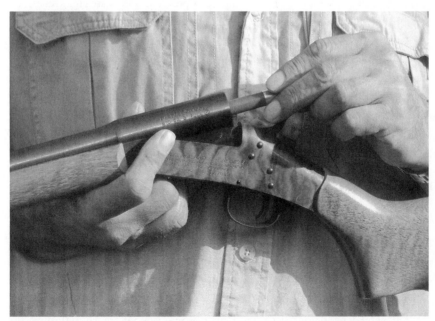

Break-open shotguns are the easiest to load, unload, and check. This is a New England Firearms .410 single-shot.

manual safety devices tend to lock the trigger mechanisms, not the firing pins. This means that if the guns are struck hard enough on either end, an "inertia firing event" can occur when the firing pin is thrown forward of its own weight, striking the shell's primer hard enough to discharge the shell in the chamber ahead of it. The result is, BANG!

This is why, across the generations of law enforcement, police shotguns have been kept "cruiser ready," which means that the tubular magazine is loaded but the firing chamber is empty. If the shotgun was stored transversely along the front seat with a shell in the chamber, and the cruiser was T-boned or spun out and hit a tree sideways, the forces could slam the firing pin forward inside its channel without the trigger even being involved, and with a round in the chamber – BANG. If the gun was racked upright in the popular dashboard rack with a shell in the chamber, and in the course of a high speed pursuit the vehicle went over a curbing or the edge of a ditch and became airborne, when it came back down and hit, those forces would bounce the firing pin upward inside that vertical shotgun and – BANG. If the shotgun was stored in the trunk of the cruiser, perhaps with its muzzle oriented toward driver or passenger, and the police vehicle was rear-ended hard – BANG.

Know thy shotgun. The break-open, breech-loading shotgun typified by the ancient double barrel design is probably the easiest and the safest to clear. Press the release lever and "break" the gun open. The shells are right there, visible and palpable: the simplest of all administrative checking, loading, or unloading.

Slide actions and semiautomatics can be more complicated, particularly once a round has been chambered. This writer learned decades ago that no one exact protocol works on every shotgun. In both the law enforcement and the self-defense markets, the two dominant brands of slide-action shotguns have for decades been the Remington Model 870 and the Mossberg Models 500 and 590. Due to their design features, they unload differently.

With a fully loaded Remington, the protocol this writer teaches is to put the muzzle in a safe direction and, with the trigger-blocking manual safety button at the rear of the trigger guard "on safe," press the slide release at the front of the trigger guard and slowly retract the slide. The chambered shell will eject; catch it in your hand or let it go to the ground to be retrieved later. The next shell in line will be sitting on the shell lift, ready to be carried into the firing chamber by the next forward stroke on the slide. Instead, roll the gun onto its ejection port side and let that shell roll out of the port. Leaving the slide to the rear, which keeps the bolt back and the ejection port open, reach in through the loading port and press the shell release at the rear of the magazine tube. This will allow the shells to pop out under spring pressure, and into your hand. Repeat until the gun is completely unloaded, its action open, and check by sight and feel to make sure.

With a fully loaded Mossberg slide action shotgun, unloading works better when the procedure is reversed. Make sure the top tang thumb safety is to the rear, "on safe." Then, we'll unload the magazine before we clear the chamber. If we try to unload it the same way as the Remington, the shell lifting mechanism will get in the way of the operator's fingers. So, on the Mossberg, we'll keep the muzzle in a safe direction as we unload every shell from the magazine, one by one just as with the Remington. Then, we'll press upward on the slide release lever at the rear of the trigger guard and slowly bring the slide back, until the "shell up the spout" comes out of the chamber through the ejection port.

The Ithaca Model 37 shotgun, once popular with police and always popular among the general public, is also best cleared magazine first, then chamber. As noted previously, know thy shotgun. Remember that most iterations of the Ithaca 37 will fire spontaneously if the slide is closed with a live shell in the chamber if the shooter's finger is holding the trigger back. The same is true of some old Winchesters, such as the Model 12 and the Model 1897.

RIFLES

Any rifle with a box magazine is best unloaded by removing the magazine (and putting the magazine in a pocket or elsewhere, so that hand is unencumbered for further manipulation of the firearm, which may still have a loaded chamber). Now, the bolt is carefully retracted to extract the chambered cartridge, which is then cleared from the rifle.

When checking by feel, IF THE RIFLE HAS BEEN RECENTLY FIRED, DO NOT insert a finger into the chamber to check by feel. High-powered rifles operate at very high pressure and can leave the firing chamber hot enough to burn human flesh. This is also true of fully automatic weapons, even submachine guns chambered for relatively low-pressure pistol cartridges.

Remember that the vast majority of rifles, irrespective of action type, do not have internal firing pin stop mechanisms that would render them drop safe. If you have ever cleared a live cartridge out of the chamber of an AR15, M16, or M4 rifle, you have probably noticed a tiny dimple on the primer that wasn't there before. It's the result of the firing pin bouncing forward in its channel when the bolt was closed to chamber that round. It hasn't hit the primer hard enough to set it off and discharge the round, but that could change with a sufficiently violent impact. If the same rifle was inside a police car (or your car)

Locked open on empty magazine, this Springfield M1A rifle can be safely chamber-checked with finger if the gun is cold, but if recently fired, DON'T. High-power .308 Winchester/7.62mm NATO ammo will make chamber area hot enough to burn finger.

As noted in the classic Ten Commandments of Firearms Safety, a manual safety is not the be all and end all of firearms accident prevention. This AR15 is "on safe."

and then subjected to the tremendous inertial forces of a collision as mentioned above in the shotgun discussion, such a rifle could discharge through inertia fire without the trigger being touched.

This is why cops don't keep their patrol rifles in their vehicles with rounds chambered; they are kept "cruiser ready" like shotguns, with chamber empty and full magazine locked in place. In the same vein, most military forces of the world leave their chambers empty, with the warfighters instructed to only put a round in the chamber when contact with the enemy is reasonably believed to be imminent or at least likely.

Likewise, smart outfitters and hunting guides have long advised their clients to leave their hunting rifles chamber-empty when on horseback, and urged them to chamber a round only when game was sighted. The reason is that most hunting rifles, including most lever action and bolt action arms, don't have secured firing pins either. Should the hunter drop the rifle from horseback, the gun may fall far enough that landing on the muzzle or the butt will impart sufficient force to create a firing pin inertia discharge. Even if the rifle is secured in a saddle scabbard, if the horse should fall the guide doesn't want the rifle in the scabbard to discharge.

While we're on that topic, we should address the fact that a bolt action rifle can be "un-cocked" or "de-cocked" safely by holding the bolt handle up, holding the trigger back, and then slowly closing the bolt handle downward into its locked position. Doing this with a round in the chamber was quite common among both professional hunters and their clients back in the days when this writer went on safaris on the African Continent.

That said, I can't endorse the practice with a round in the chamber. Many of those African veterans considered it safe; the hunter would quietly raise and then lower the bolt handle to cock the gun for the already-chambered round. Gunsmiths have assured me that in the un-cocked mode, the rifle's striker (firing pin) can still be subject to inertia fire. Better to follow the model of the American West: chamber empty until target sighted.

HANDGUNS

Being shorter than rifles or shotguns, handguns can more easily be pointed in improper directions. They are normally carried on the body for longer periods of time, creating greater exposure to potential mishaps.

A significant percentage of handgun accidents come during holstering and drawing the gun from the holster. In the old days, most holsters exposed the trigger guard, and the pattern of accident was that the finger would get on the trigger too early, something would snag the gun during the draw, the gun and its trigger would stop but the hand and its finger would keep moving and there would be an unexpected BANG.

In hopes of curing this, the holster industry began covering the trigger guards. This did indeed go far to preventing that type of accident. Unfortunately, in the end, it also had the effect of redistributing the pattern of unintended discharge. Now, the accidents happened during the holstering process, not during the draw. The shooter would leave the finger on the trigger, the finger would hit the edge of the holster and stop, the gun and trigger would keep going and, once again, there would be the BANG.

Ergo, as noted earlier, the rationale for the holstering process I pioneered even before establishing Lethal Force Institute in 1981. Trigger finger STRAIGHT, which everyone else was already recommending anyway, and ALSO thumb on hammer area. This held the double action gun's hammer down, so it couldn't rise or fall without the thumb feeling it in time to stop an unintended discharge. It held the cocked and locked single action auto pistol's hammer back, so if something tripped the trigger, the thumb could catch it and block its fall. This also took the web of the hand off any existing grip safety, activating that part's safety function, yet another layer of safety.

With a striker-fired pistol that has no hammer per se, the thumb on the back still serves good purposes. It makes the shooter a better role model for others whose guns WILL be safer when holstered this way. It keeps his own gun's slide in battery; a striker-fired gun's slide comes back more easily than one whose slide is held forward by a mainspring-loaded hammer. This means that in a new or too-tight holster, the slide can be pushed out of battery during

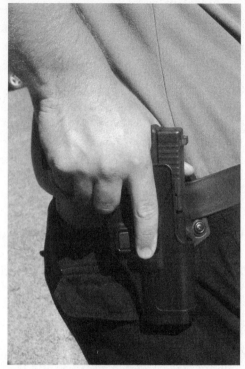

With the popular SERPA and similar holsters, author counsels pressing release paddle with fingerPRINT, not fingerTIP!

the insertion process, rendering the gun unshootable, as there is no guarantee that the tight holster will pull the slide back INTO battery during the draw. This holstering method guarantees that every auto pistol will be ready to shoot and defend its owner's life when it comes out of the scabbard on the shortest possible notice.

One popular holster style today, pioneered and typified by the Blackhawk SERPA, holds the gun secure with a lock released by pressing inward on a paddle or button with the trigger finger. It is our nature to press buttons with the tip of our finger. This points the finger inward as the gun clears the holster, and allows the fingertip to slide in, putting the index finger on the trigger prematurely. Accidental discharges resulting from this are not, in my opinion, a fault of the holster, but of the user. The paddle or button needs to be depressed with the flat part of the distal phalange of the trigger finger. The easy way to remember it is this: FINGERPRINT, NOT FINGERTIP!

Holstering protocols are covered more thoroughly in Gun Digest Book of Concealed Carry than what I'm allowed space for here. A brief recap, however:

With a hip holster, click your heels together like a German soldier when you're holstering and tilt your upper body away from the holster: that points the muzzle farther away from your lower limbs. (Credit: master instructor David Maglio.) With an appendix holster, lean back at the hips; this puts the muzzle more out in front of you and away from the genital and femoral artery areas. (Credit: master instructor Phil Wong.) With a horizontal or vertical upside-down shoulder holster, keep the muzzle in a safe direction and turn your body to bring the holster to the gun, keeping the arm on that side raised and clear of the muzzle as the gun goes into the holster.

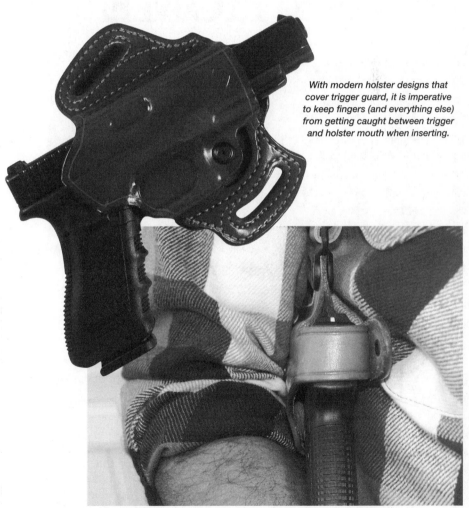

With modern holster designs that cover trigger guard, it is imperative to keep fingers (and everything else) from getting caught between trigger and holster mouth when inserting.

Although this Kahr pistol is perfectly safe encompassed in this left-handed shoulder holster, its muzzle points to the rear, which will alarm some people who see it.

CHAPTER TWO

FIREARMS STORAGE IN THE HOME

A top-quality gun safe like this one is a valuable component of safe firearms storage.

Biometric quick-access gun safe has opened immediately for THIS user, but author has found some people who just aren't compatible with biometrics.

Safe home firearms storage breaks down into two categories: simple storage and defensive-ready storage.

SIMPLE STORAGE

Simple storage is what we do with the target shooter's pistol, the outdoorsman's revolver, the hunter's rifle or shotgun. It is stored under

Author demonstrates quick release of loaded pistol inside Gun Vault.

lock and key, the key in question being available only to one or more people who have been pre-identified as logical, sound-minded individuals. Ammunition is stored in a separate location, ideally also under lock and key. For the hobbyist who has no intention of ever reaching for the gun in defense of self or others during a life-threatening emergency, Simple Storage makes sense.

A good quality safe is the best bet for this type of storage. Speed of access will not be an issue. It accomplishes a cornerstone objective: keeping the gun(s) out of the hands of those

This quick access safe from Gun Vault is designed to guide fingers into position for push-button combination release in the dark. Notice the key lock over-ride, important in case batteries fail. Obviously, key should not be left in lock with loaded gun inside and unattended.

who should not have access to firearms. This includes irresponsible youngsters, equally irresponsible adults, and assorted burglars and other evildoers who might break into your home with hostile intent.

DEFENSIVE-READY STORAGE

Defensive-ready storage puts a loaded gun quickly into the hand of the person defending self and loved ones against a home invasion. Quick access to authorized hands now becomes a cornerstone priority. A gun unloaded in one locked location and ammunition locked in another location is a fine plan for simple storage, but it's simply impossible to bring the two together in time to interdict a fast-breaking home invasion. We can't alter the time/space continuum with wishful thinking.

To keep the gun securely locked yet readily accessible requires a quick-release gun safe. There are several on the market. Some use biometrics. At this writing, you'll have to test them to see if they work for you. The history of biometrics so far is that some people's hands are simply incompatible with the technology. For me, the test unit worked pretty well. For my significant other, it often failed. Conclusion: for us, at this level of its development, the technology just wasn't going to work.

Even if it had worked as well for her as for me under perfect test conditions, I still would have been leery of it. When it has to recognize your fingerprints, what's the effect of a Band-Aid on your finger that obscures your fingerprint? Or blood from a struggle after you broke free from the assailant and ran for the gun? Or dirt in the whorls of your fingerprints if you were in the garden when you heard the screaming child being attacked by a vicious dog?

In my book The Truth About Self-Protection (Police Bookshelf, PO Box 122, Concord, NH 03302), I talked about tests I did more than thirty years ago. We simply timed how long it would take for me, in the intruder role, to get to the farthest room in the house once I had breached the front door. We then timed how long it would take the homeowner to go from various rooms to where the gun was, and get it out of the storage container. The results, when correlated, were not encouraging.

What was ALWAYS the fastest for the homeowner – the ultimate, most efficient method of Defensive-Ready Storage – was for the householder to already be carrying a loaded handgun on their person.

This does not mean that the homeowner has to strap on a Buscadero cowboy belt and a big six-shooter or two every moment they are at home. It can be something as simple as a small handgun carried concealed in the pants pocket or in an ankle holster, or a larger gun holstered inside the waistband under an un-tucked shirt. It won't frighten the postman or the UPS man or the kid selling Girl Scout Cookies who comes unexpectedly to the front door, but is immediately accessible the moment someone kicks in your door. Imagine the horror of suddenly finding a homicidal intruder already in your house after he has surreptitiously gained entry, and having to cross his path to get to your firearm.

The choice is yours. So is the responsibility for your safety and that of your family. Looking back over atrocities ranging from the massacre of the Clutter family in Kansas documented in Truman Capote's best-selling book In Cold Blood to the much more recent slaughter of the Petit family in Cheshire, Connecticut, there would have been no time for any of the victims to run to a gun safe. But, reconstruction shows that, if any of the adults present had been carrying concealed weapons, they would have had ample opportunity to turn the tables and save their own lives, and the lives of their children, from the monsters who murdered them.

"SMART GUNS"

There has been much talk of "smart guns," which only fire in the hands of their legitimate users and forbid unauthorized hands from unleashing their firepower. It's a great idea, but for the most part, it's a classic example of magical thinking. The reason is that it is what engineers call vaporware: it exists in theory, but has not been proven in the real world, with one notable exception.

Smart guns that recognize fingerprints biometrically? We've had the discussion already. Biometrics remains far from 100% for emergency life-saving equipment such as defensive firearms. Radio signals from a transmitter worn on the designated user's body? Totally unproven as yet.

The one smart gun that actually works has been with us since the mid-1970s, the Magna-Trigger device invented by the late Joe Smith and now available through Rick Devoid at Tarnhelm (www.tarnhelm.com). This is a modification of a medium-size (K-frame) or larger Smith & Wesson revolver which allows it to only be fired in the hand of a designated user wearing a special magnetic ring on the middle finger. This writer thought it was BS in the late 1970s and sacrificed a Smith & Wesson Model 66 .357 revolver to prove it. However, torture testing proved the device to work remarkably well. From the time my oldest child was three years old, that was the gun I kept at bedside fully loaded. Now that I have grandchildren, it's on standby if they come to visit.

Despite great efforts to do so, the concept has never been effectively adapted to the semiautomatic pistols police were switching to from revolvers when the Magna-Trigger came out. That's why it never became widely popular. However, it's still available, and an excellent answer to the question, "How do I keep a defense gun loaded and ready to quickly grab, without worrying about the kids getting hold of it or the bad guys taking it away from me and shooting me with it?"